Havens of Hope

Havens *of* Hope

Ideas for Redesigning Education from the COVID-19 Pandemic

By Shira Leibowitz, PhD

Redleaf Press®
www.redleafpress.org
800-423-8309

Published by Redleaf Press
10 Yorkton Court
St. Paul, MN 55117
www.redleafpress.org

First edition 2022
Cover design by Erin Kirk
Cover photograph by Irina Tkachuk/stock.adobe.com
Interior design by Michelle Lee Lagerroos
Typeset in Arno Pro, Futura PT, and Miller Text
Interior illustrations by Liliia/stock.adobe.com
Printed in the United States of America
29 28 27 26 25 24 23 22 1 2 3 4 5 6 7 8 9

Library of Congress Cataloging-in-Publication Data

Names: Leibowitz, Shira, author.
Title: Havens of hope : ideas for redesigning education from the COVID-19 pandemic / by Shira Leibowitz.
Description: First edition. | St. Paul, MN : Redleaf Press, 2022. | Summary: "This book shares the hopeful energy and positive transformation that is emerging through the early childhood education field in this historic time of pandemic, economic uncertainty, and protests for racial equity. It brings readers on a journey into the possibility for new approaches in education to learning emerging in response to the momentous challenges of our times"-- Provided by publisher.
Identifiers: LCCN 2021059944 (print) | LCCN 2021059945 (ebook) | ISBN 9781605547619 (paperback) | ISBN 9781605547626 (ebook)
Subjects: LCSH: Early childhood education--United States. | Educational change--United States. | Social distancing (Public health) and education--United States. | COVID-19 Pandemic, 2020-
Classification: LCC LB1139.25 .L44 2022 (print) | LCC LB1139.25 (ebook) | DDC 372.210973--dc23/eng/20220106
LC record available at https://lccn.loc.gov/2021059944
LC ebook record available at https://lccn.loc.gov/2021059945
Printed on acid-free paper

Contents

Acknowledgments

To the many educators, families, and children throughout the world who, through times of tremendous adversity, made the impossible possible, creating havens of hope in a world in need of so much healing.

With appreciation and thanks to the educators, families, and children of my very own Discovery Village Childcare and Preschool in Tarrytown, New York,

and

with gratitude to those who gave their time and wisdom to share their inspiring stories with me:

Acton Academy Silicon Valley, Belmont, California
Maria Ferrari, cofounder and head of operations

Beacon Hebrew Alliance Preschool, Beacon, New York
Ilana Friedman, director and lead teacher

Boulder Journey School, Boulder, Colorado
Alex Morgan, community outreach specialist
Lauren Weatherly, partner school program director
Alison Maher, executive director
Andrea Sisbarro, school director

Building Blocks Preschool, Highland, Michigan
Suzanne Gabli, owner

Discovery Child Care Centre, Barrie, Ontario, Canada
Jessica Holder, pedagogical leader
Karen Eilersen, founder and owner

Emergent Expressions, Peru
Kaitlin Coppola, founder

Farmingdale School District, Farmingdale, New York
Dr. William Brennan, assistant superintendent for innovation and organizational development

Hope Day School, Dallas, Texas
Cori Berg, executive director

Hudson Lab School, Hastings-on-Hudson, New York
Cate Han, founder
Stacey Seltzer, cofounder
Joanne Corrigan, intergenerational program coordinator

Inspiring New Perspectives, Waltham, Massachusetts
Susan MacDonald, founder

Kaleidoscope Community School, Salem, Oregon
Ashley Acers, owner/founder
Molly Brown, director

Koala Park Daycare, Tuckahoe, New York
Karina Wyllie, owner

Larchmont Charter School, Los Angeles, California
Sara Lev, transitional kindergarten teacher

Muck and Wonder Farm School, Sacramento, California
Jenna Maggard, director
Jess Durrett, parent of a Muck and Wonder Farm School student

My Reflection Matters Village, Waterbury Connecticut
Chemay Morales-James, founder
Tamsyn Ambler, member
Cecilia Cruz Brooks, member
Dominique DjeDje, member

Preschool System and Preschool All Stars Membership
Joy Anderson, owner

Randolph School, Wappingers Falls, New York
Josh Kaplan, director

Santa Clara Unified School District, Parent Participation Preschool, Santa Clara, California
Josiane Sawaya, teacher

Sunbeam Nature School, Petaluma, California
Shawna Thompson, founding director

Temple Beth Shalom, Needham, Massachusetts
Rachel Happel, director of K–12 learning
Sarah Damelin, program director

The Open School, Santa Ana, California
Cassandra Clausen, founder

Tomorrow's Promise, The Montessori School of Huntsville, Huntsville, Texas
Kaye Boehning, director

White Dove Montessori, Plano, Texas
Nelum Walpola, directress

Windsor Hill Primary School, Falmouth, Maine
Mary Roux Train, cofounder and teacher

Part One

Beginnings

Introduction

COVID-19 and the Start of Something New

Standing in the only open room at the child care center and preschool I had begun less than a year earlier, I wondered: Were we experiencing a founding moment for education, the start of something new? COVID-19 had changed everything. And not only in the obvious ways.

Long faulted for being painfully slow to change, schools transformed, literally overnight. Many did it exceptionally well. Not only were we navigating through a global pandemic and managing—we were getting better. The process was messy and full of challenges. Yet we were not only improving incrementally, as is typical in schools, even schools of excellence. We were improving exponentially, accomplishing what we had never before imagined possible. It was both a time of despair and a time of renewal.

It wasn't the first time that crisis had fueled educational rebirth. The Montessori, Waldorf, and Reggio-inspired approaches to learning were all born out of the turbulence and despair of twentieth-century Europe. Maria Montessori encountered gender and economic inequity in turn-of-the-century Italy. Rudolf Steiner, founder of the Waldorf approach, was deeply influenced by the devastation Germany suffered in the aftermath of World War I. Loris Malaguzzi, who pioneered what has come to be known as Reggio-inspired learning, experienced the brutal oppression and destruction of World War II.

The messages of all three of these educational founders resonated deeply, reaching across continents and generations. I never imagined that I might one day live through events even remotely as consequential. Yet here I was, running a child care center and preschool in 2020 in downstate New York, one of the first and worst COVID-19 hotspots in the United States. Deemed essential in many states, including New York, child care programs were allowed and even encouraged to remain open even as schools and most businesses were required to shut down or operate remotely. K–12 schools and numerous early childhood programs moved immediately online, continuing to serve although they could not remain physically open.

From the very beginning of the pandemic, I chose for my child care center and preschool, Discovery Village in Tarrytown, New York, to remain open. Initially only a tiny number of children of essential workers attended. I decided also to provide free remote learning for my students who remained at home during those first frightening months of the pandemic. I implemented COVID-19 health protocols before there was guidance on how to do so, while functioning with essentially no income. Just weeks earlier, the thought of all of this would have sounded like a bizarre dystopian novel. And yet I was doing it.

I wasn't alone. Throughout the country and throughout the world educators and families weren't only surviving—we were rapidly improving, adapting to be present for our students in the ways they needed us, serving as havens of hope in a world in need of so much healing. This book shares some of our stories.

On the surface, this is a book about COVID, written in real time as the educators I interviewed and I were navigating through daunting challenges and adversity. Yet delving deeper, it's not so much a book about COVID at all. It's far more a reflection on what is possible for our learning and for our lives when we set our minds to saying "yes" to possibility.

During the COVID-19 pandemic, educators, parents, and children made the impossible possible. If we did it once, because we had to, we can do it again because we choose to. We can redesign learning to reflect our visions for our children and for our world.

As you read, I welcome you to view yourself in these pages. Consider how you design learning and care that resonates with your own vision and values while remaining responsive to the realities of those you teach, lead, and care for. I invite you to join in conversation and collaboration with many others who are charting their own course forward, designing schools and other educational programs that stand out by virtue of what they stand for.

I welcome you to see yourself in the pages of this book; your own work, sense of purpose and possibility, and responses to adversity. Rather than merely reading, I invite you to consider ways of applying the insights in this book to redesign learning in your own school or organization. You can access these resources to support you in the process for free at https://revabilities.com/books-by-shira-leibowitz. You're also welcome to email me at shira@revabilities.com. I'd love to hear from you!

Northern Italy, 1945

It had been only five days since World War II ended. Women and men, young and old, farmers and factory workers from the tiny working-class village of Villa Cella, in the Reggio Emilia province of northern Italy, banded together. Their village lay in ruins. The entire region, a stronghold of the Italian resistance, had suffered. The area had endured relentless bombing by the British and brutal attacks by Italian fascist forces. But, amid the devastation, there was love and hope.

Faced with rebuilding their lives, villagers showed rare vision as they focused not merely on surviving but on setting a strong foundation for the future. Using land donated by a farmer, stones and bricks from bombed-out buildings, and funding from the sale of a tank, three trucks, and a few horses abandoned by the German forces, they set out to build a preschool. They wanted quality learning and care for their children in the present, but they also sought to prepare the next generation to stand strong against the oppression, injustice, and inequity they were certain would arise again.

Hearing rumors about the preschool, twenty-five-year-old educator Loris Malaguzzi hopped onto his bicycle and rode to Villa Cella to see what was happening. Encountering mothers collecting materials to build their school, he introduced himself as a teacher. With that, they invited him to teach their children. Eight months later, The April 25th School, named in honor of Liberation Day, opened, with thirty young students in the pioneering class. In the following months, years, and decades, Malaguzzi inspired many other schools throughout the surrounding area, the province, the country, and, in time, the world. Reggio-inspired schools are hailed for their child-centered, relationship-based, experiential approach to learning. Less frequently celebrated is the grounding of the approach in that founding moment in Villa Cella. Bricks and love, stones and hope, sweat and the fiercely fought-for values of tolerance, justice, and equity set a foundation for the future.

Seventy-Five Years Later

It was the spring of 2020, only months since the first case of COVID-19. With a rapidly rising death toll globally, nonessential businesses as well as K–12 schools and universities in many parts of the world ceased all in-person operations. Economic uncertainty and massive unemployment followed. Child care centers, which in most places were deemed essential, were typically allowed, and even encouraged, to remain open. In the following months, egregious acts of brutality against people of color led to widespread protests for racial equity. Destructive weather events brought wreckage throughout the world. Teaching in an environment of such pain and despair, whether remotely or in person, took a heavy toll.

But amid the devastation, there was love and hope. Teachers and families banded together, seeking ways to care for and teach children in the frightening, uncertain environment in which we found ourselves. Conversations extended across countries and continents. Remembering past stories of hope in the face of crises that had birthed new educational approaches, some wondered: Might we be facing a moment similar to that experienced by the villagers of Villa Cella, Italy? Might the challenges we were facing fuel new possibilities for learning? The months, years, and decades lying ahead called to us. What gifts, what qualities of character might we instill in our children to help strengthen and prepare them for the challenges their futures might hold? What wisdom did the experiences of our own times have to offer?

Perhaps we were standing at a beginning, on the cusp of something new.

1

Founding Moments

The moment it first occurred to me that I might personally be experiencing a founding moment for education was at once mundane and powerful.

It was April 2020, and I was with the children in the only open classroom at Discovery Village Childcare and Preschool, the child care center I had started less than a year earlier in Tarrytown, New York. Only two out of more than twenty staff members were with me. The rest I sadly had to furlough, at least temporarily. Only six out of more than eighty children had come to school. The rest were at home with their families, adhering to the state's shelter-in-place order. Ten out of the center's eleven classrooms remained dark, silent, and empty.

But in our one open room, we were having fun. Two of our preschoolers were taking apart a farm they had made from cardboard boxes and repurposing the boxes to build a car wash. A third preschooler transformed the cardboard road to their farm into a road that led anywhere you wanted to vacation, real or imaginary. He then invited everyone, children and adults alike, to drive the spanking-clean toy cars coming out of the car wash down what he called his highway to happiness.

The remaining three toddlers were giving baths to toy animals, former residents of the now abandoned farm. They used individual bins filled with water and soapsuds. Before COVID-19, children had enjoyed sharing huge bins to explore a wide variety of materials. With COVID-19 we could no longer have many children touching the same materials. The switch to individual bins was seamless, and children were delighted to have their own materials.

The focus on washing, both cars and animals, emerged from our constant handwashing, a core component of our COVID-19 health and safety protocols. Between every activity, and at least every half hour, children washed their hands. Going to the sink and washing our hands became the punctuation mark of our days, offering a moment of respite during transitions.

Children had so much fun savoring the feel of water and soapsuds as they washed their hands that we filled their individual bins with soap and water. Our kids took it from there; creating a car wash, a highway for those clean cars, and bathtubs for their animals. They were, quite literally, cleansing their worlds, washing the animals and cars they so loved as well as their own precious hands. Simultaneously, they were opening their minds to the possible, creating their own highway to happiness, imagining where they wanted to go in the moment and well into the future.

In the following weeks, our children's curiosity about water brought us in many new directions. We explored the depths of the sea and designed our own aquarium. We looked to the rain clouds above, showering our world with water, and built our own cloud observatory. We marveled at the power of water to nourish plants and people and tended an indoor garden. As we lost ourselves in our playful learning, the outside world melted away. It was as if each day we entered our very own island of calm, our very own haven of hope.

We did not take the environment of playful calm and hopeful possibility we were creating for granted. It is hard to recapture the fear and intensity of those days.

We were located in downstate New York, at the time among the worst COVID-19 hotspots in the world, so the health threats were terrifyingly real. Awakening each day feeling healthy was a tremendous blessing. While a far second from health concerns, financial threats also loomed large. The cost of remaining open for so few children was higher than the cost of closing. How long I could hang on financially was a very real worry. Health and hope became my guiding wishes. I began ending messages to people with the words "stay healthy and hopeful."

Like Dorothy in *The Wizard of Oz*, I felt as if I had gone to sleep in one reality and awoken in another. Everything was at once different and the same. I alternately imagined myself as a character in a historical fiction novel; a time traveler returning to a past age; an immigrant in a new land, although I had never actually left home; a survivor in a dystopian reality; and an avatar in a video game. Embracing my tiny role in an unfolding global saga as an owner of a small business, a child care center and preschool deemed essential, I committed to doing everything possible to serve our families and children. I also reached out in fellowship to other child care centers. Having learned much about Small Business Administration loans, I guided other center owners through the process of applying for federal funding.

I not only wanted to remain physically open, I also wanted to reach out to the families and children who had suspended enrollment and were sheltering in place at home. Initially it felt ludicrous to even consider remote learning for preschoolers, toddlers, and especially infants. Yet we stretched our thinking, opening ourselves to possibilities we had never previously imagined. Soon those new options felt not only possible but even routine.

I began by sending electronic messages with activities families could enjoy together at home, conveying messages of hope. Teachers created videos of themselves leading songs, stories, exercise, and dance. Within a few short weeks, we were providing real-time learning opportunities via video conferencing, including greetings and socializing, circle time with literacy and math activities, exercise, Spanish and sign language classes, and active games. With resilience and creativity, we were rapidly adapting.

Throughout it all, I noticed something I hadn't anticipated. My center was getting better. We were not merely making incremental enhancements. While facing the worst of times, we were dramatically improving. It was as though crisis ignited the best of ourselves, empowering us to uncover and apply our deepest values and highest qualities of our character to our work.

The memory of a photo I had once seen of the Villa Cella families physically building the first Reggio preschool emerged in my mind's eye. For a moment it was as if I were standing in Italy in 1945. My heart stirred as I thought about those preschoolers. They were now in their late seventies, perhaps still living in northern Italy, which was, at the time, among the first and worst COVID-19 hotspots in the world. I prayed they were well while worrying they might not be.

I took a deep breath and uttered a quiet prayer, acknowledging my arrival at a personal founding moment, the possibility of the start of something new. I then set out to connect with others who I anticipated might be on a similar journey.

The Power of Dialogue: Boulder Journey School

With a few social media posts in April 2020, I connected with early childhood educators throughout the world. We joined together on video conferences, sharing our experiences and offering one another connection and support.

Through the outreach I quickly became acquainted with a force in the world of early childhood education. Boulder Journey School in Colorado stood out as a nexus point, uniting many on a journey of connection. Gracious and proactive, Alex Morgan, the community outreach specialist for the school, reached out to me. She shared that she and her colleague Lauren Weatherly, the partner school program director, were facilitating weekly virtual conversations with hundreds of early childhood educators throughout the world. Alex welcomed me to join, offering a breakout room where I could facilitate conversation with educators who were interested in focusing on the birth of new educational approaches in an age of pandemic.

I was by no means the only educator Alex and Lauren contacted. As fear and a profound sense of isolation gripped the early childhood world during the beginning weeks of the pandemic, Alex and Lauren were on a mission. They checked in with graduates of the master's program Boulder Journey School runs in collaboration with the University of Colorado Denver, as well as with educators who had toured the school or participated in their professional development workshops. Alex and Lauren found a longing for connection. In response, within the first two weeks of the pandemic, they launched what would become weekly conversations. Within just twenty-four hours, they received six hundred RSVPs from educators throughout the world signing on to their virtual dialogues.

Boulder Journey School leveraged a small number of high-impact strengths to make a profound difference for the field of early childhood education. These included a substantial network of educators who have learned there, expertise in facilitating adult learning, and credibility with the adult learners its educators serve by virtue of being in the trenches just like them, running an early childhood program. Educators at the school also have an impressive ability to listen and understand the needs of those in their network. "We found just how powerful it is for people to come together and just talk," Alex explained.

Virtual conversations were not the only meaningful contribution Boulder Journey School brought to the field during the beginning challenging days of the pandemic. Offering an online master's program had been a dream for the school prior to the pandemic. The school's leadership had laid much of the groundwork, and when the pandemic hit, they accelerated their efforts and were able quickly to launch their online master's program. Hoping to recruit twenty-five students, the school leaders were surprised and overjoyed to enroll seventy-seven students in its pioneering cohort. Previous concerns leaders had about the quality they would be able to offer in an online learning model quickly abated. A great strength was the diversity of the international cohort of students who enrolled. "The quality of international dialogue surpassed all expectations," executive director Alison Maher shared.

While Boulder Journey School stood out as exemplary in nurturing connections, it was not alone. Throughout the world, educators were reaching out to one another. The relationships forged in those early months of the pandemic set a foundation that would assist us as we were again shaken to our core.

From Pandemic to Protest

The murder of George Floyd on May 25, 2020, left millions horrified and heartbroken. It was too painful to bear; a Black man, accused of using a counterfeit bill, murdered by a white police officer who knelt on his neck for more than nine minutes despite multiple pleas for air, for breath, for life. Protests erupted, locally, nationally, and globally.

Outrage at the most brutal, egregious actions against people of color gave way to self-reflection on bias and racism in our own spheres of influence. We were called to look inward, recognizing oppression and inequity in our society. Many owned the need to incorporate ways of honestly facing racism and bias into our educational approaches. Again, Boulder Journey School offered a model for how early childhood educators might respond, prepared through its longtime focus on promoting anti-racism and antibias education as well as through the experience of facilitating virtual conversations with educators.

"We found new courage to meet families in ways we hadn't before," Alex explained. They opened weekly virtual dialogues with families and faculty on the topic of anti-racism that continued through the summer. Families embraced the opportunity, seeking connection with others and wanting so much to speak. Staff reviewed curricular materials, administrative practices, and professional development programming so as to further embed equity and anti-racist and antibias learning within the school.

I was pulled back, yet again, to the founding of the very first Reggio school, grounded in its commitment to prepare children to stand strong against injustice, inequity, and oppression. Seventy-five years and an ocean apart, we were again seeking ways to stand strong against our own era's injustice, inequity, and oppression.

Meanwhile, our need for connection throughout the months of pandemic and protest remained palpable. We continued to reach out to one another for support.

As I became ever more immersed in conversations with educators, I was continuously awed. Not only were we navigating through challenges and adversity we had never previously imagined; we were refining our visions and approaches to learning. And it wasn't only one vision or only one new approach emerging. There were many.

I wondered: Might we be witnessing the beginning of multiple new approaches to learning? Even before families in Villa Cella built the first Reggio school, the Montessori and Waldorf educational approaches had emerged on the European landscape and then spread globally. Might those experiences and approaches, their similarities and their differences, hold wisdom for us?

Montessori

I took a brief respite from the contemporary pulls on me, looking back in time, seeking guidance. My first stop was Rome, in 1907. Although Italy was experiencing economic and social revitalization, inequity abounded, and many lived in extreme poverty. The San Lorenzo quarter of Rome was among the most destitute, described as the shame of Italy. Crime there was so extreme that it is said even the local police were afraid to enter the neighborhood.

Amid the devastation, a group of wealthy bankers sought economic gain. They took over an abandoned, unfinished skeleton of a building in San Lorenzo. After minimal work, installing doors and windows, water pipes and drains, they welcomed five hundred previously homeless married couples and their children as residents.

In a neighborhood known for crime and violence, the greatest threat to the building came from an unanticipated source: a group of fifty children between the ages of two and six. Without access to child care or any familial or communal support, parents had no option but to leave their children home alone while they worked. Left unsupervised and without direction, the children did what children do: create their own fun and wreak havoc in the process.

The bankers responded decisively. All children left alone in the tenement building during the day had to stay together in one bare, empty room. They then reached out to an unlikely resource, international speaker, medical officer of hygiene, and the first female doctor in Italy, Dr. Maria Montessori.

It was hard for many to imagine what a celebrated doctor and academic would find of interest in a project involving fifty formerly homeless toddlers and preschoolers. Yet, from the start, Montessori saw the project as one of enormous potential significance. She had already made noteworthy gains offering educational interventions for children with significant cognitive and emotional challenges who had been abandoned in asylums. Eager to observe the effect of her educational approaches on typically developing children, she raised funds and hired a teacher. After providing the children with materials she believed would engage them, she observed.

In the following months, a transformation occurred. Given Montessori's carefully prepared materials and the space to explore, the children became far more social and communicative. They showed gratitude and began demonstrating pride in their surroundings. The children not only took care of their classroom but cleaned and organized their apartments, inspiring their families to tend to their own living spaces with greater care. In time, the children learned to write and then to read. This innovative approach of learning writing before reading, begun in the very first Montessori school in San Lorenzo, remains prominent in Montessori schools throughout the world today.

Inspired by the possibilities for learning she envisioned, Montessori left her medical and academic positions to open schools and mentor others in using her approach. Among the educators throughout the world Montessori personally trained was an American, Anne George, who founded the very first Montessori school in the United States. George opened her school in 1911 in Tarrytown, New York, the very town where my own child care center and preschool is located.

Standing in Tarrytown, 109 years after George opened the first Montessori school in the United States, I thought about how Montessori schools had transcended place and time, spreading throughout the world and across the generations. Could my generation be on the cusp of also founding something new? Might my own center in Tarrytown be part of a learning revival, just as George's school had been?

A visionary and an entrepreneur, Montessori had sought to ensure fidelity to her approach. Yet her ideas proved to be too influential to contain. Knowingly or even unknowingly, many non-Montessori-trained educators today incorporate approaches Maria Montessori brought to the world. With ebbs and flows in popularity over the years, devoted adherents and staunch critics, the Montessori approach has made a powerful global impact on views of learning and the child.

Living life on her own terms, Montessori designed learning as she designed her life. The first female physician in Italy and a single mother, she unapologetically opted never to marry. She left the security of prestigious medical and academic positions to chart her own course. Independence was deeply rooted in the way she chose to live her life. Entering San Lorenzo, Montessori encountered a group of children who in many ways embraced her own value of independence. Left unsupervised, they channeled their potential in unproductive directions, but placed in a nurturing environment that valued and celebrated their independence, they thrived.

The Montessori and Reggio-inspired approaches were born in values that resonated with a particular time and place yet have transcended that time and place. Reggio-inspired learning is grounded in the values of equity and justice, while the Montessori approach is anchored in a deep commitment to independence as well as living in harmony with oneself, others, and the natural world. A commitment to peace emerged over time for Montessori as she experienced the crisis and conflict of two world wars. Her expanded vision viewed young children as key to societal reform and future, long-term peace.

Waldorf

I wanted to explore further, and my next visit to twentieth-century educational founding moments was Stuttgart, Germany. It was April 1919, just five months after the end of World War I. Inflation and unemployment in defeated Germany surged, resulting in crippling poverty and hunger along with widespread social and political unrest. Yet amid the devastation, there was hope and energy.

Socially and spiritually minded Emil Molt, owner and director of the Waldorf-Astoria Cigarette Factory in Stuttgart, Germany, was starting a school for his employees' children. Molt turned to philosopher, social reformer, and literary critic Rudolf Steiner for help, and together they founded the first Waldorf school. Molt provided the funding, purchasing a restaurant in downtown Stuttgart and redesigning it as a school. Steiner provided the vision, grounded in a holistic approach to learning aimed at cultivating the intellectual, emotional, physical, and spiritual capacities of students, as well as their imagination and creativity, preparing them to contribute to the desperately needed revitalization of their nation.

The Stuttgart Waldorf School opened in September 1919 with twelve teachers and 253 children. While most students were the children of Molt's employees, about fifty children were enrolled privately by their parents. Thus, the school served children from both working- and middle-class families.

Within three years, the school grew to eleven hundred students, with many more turned away for lack of space. In 1925, the year of Steiner's death, a second Waldorf school opened in London, followed by a school in the Netherlands, and several years later, a school in New York. More schools followed. When the Nazis came to power, they closed all the German Waldorf schools, offended by Waldorf's commitment to educate children to be free and independent thinkers.

In the following years, Waldorf schools flourished across the globe. While deeply grounded in the developing spiritual life of children, Waldorf learning is embracing and inclusive, catering to individuals with wide-ranging religious and spiritual perspectives. As Montessori is steeped in independence and Reggio is grounded in justice and equity, Waldorf centers itself in a holistic approach to both learning and life. Steiner and his admirers believed that Germany's revival depended on addressing not only economic and political challenges but also cultural, social, and spiritual ones. That deep value placed on finding holistic solutions to daunting challenges and adversity transcended time and place, resonating widely. Over the years Waldorf has grown to be the largest independent school movement in the world.

Transcending Time and Place

Born out of crises in particular times and particular places, the Montessori, Waldorf, and Reggio-inspired approaches to learning have extended through the generations and across the continents. Might the powerful visions for learning emerging in the face of the daunting global challenges and adversity of the early 2020s prove strong enough to last well into the next generation? Could we join together to more actively nurture our efforts and amplify our impact? For me the first step was to discover and explore, so I immersed myself in learning about what might be emerging.

The following pages share my journey exploring a range of programs. These include

- early childhood programs, some that remained open and some that went remote;
- pods that evolved into microschools;
- schools, including public, charter, and independent; and
- innovative communities, including a synagogue that stepped in to fill in gaps where schools left off and a co-learning community primarily serving BIPOC homeschooling families.

The stories shared represent only an infinitesimal sampling of the experiences of educators and families throughout the 2019–2020 and 2020–2021 academic years. Many of us not only navigated through the crises we faced but found ways to become ever better versions of ourselves. We can learn from the experiences so that moving forward we can bring to life our powerful visions for learning even—or perhaps especially—in the face of daunting challenges and adversity. We can find ways to stand out as ever better versions of ourselves, grounded in the values and vision that reflect what we stand for.

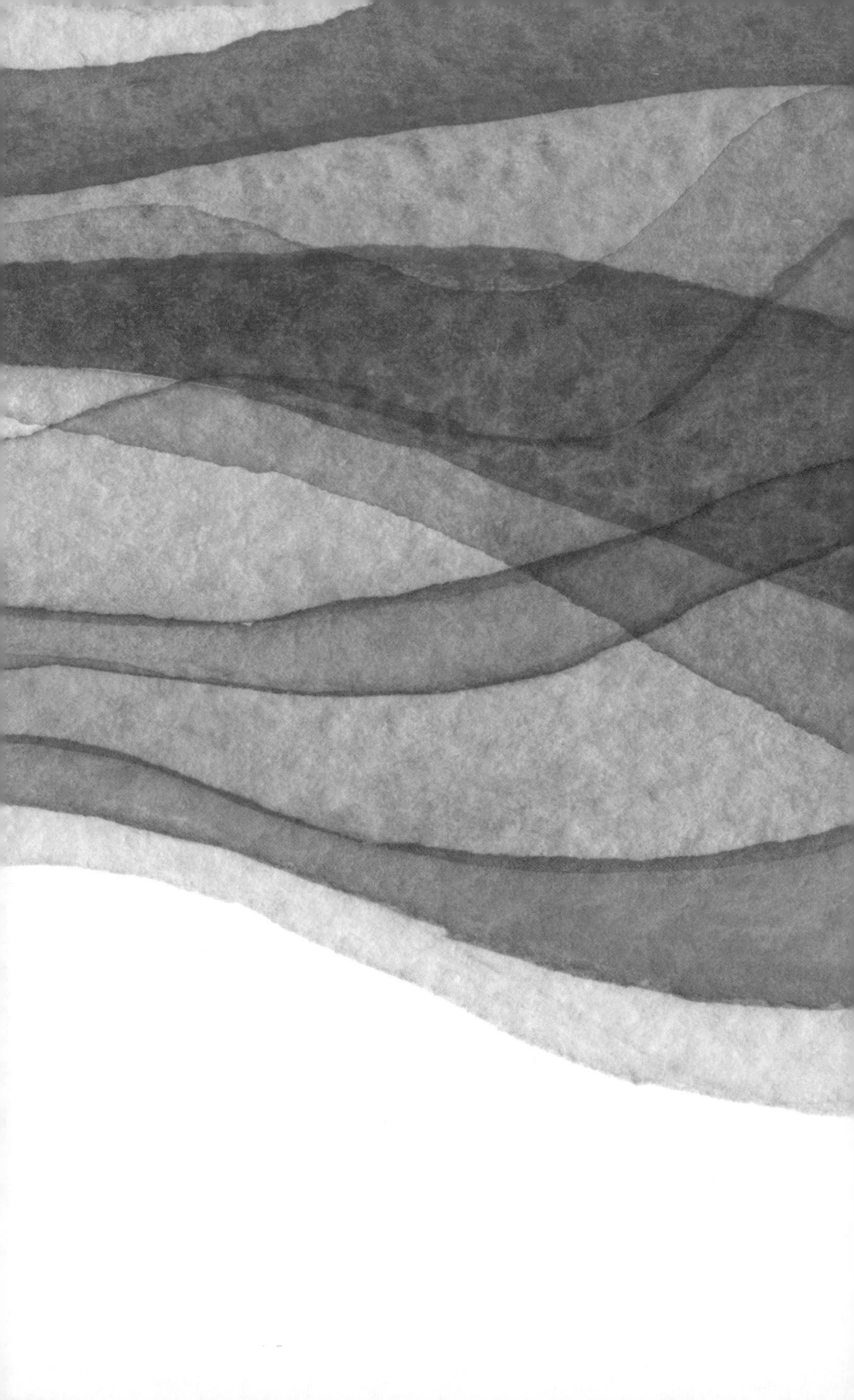

Part Two

Adversity and Possibility

2

Early Childhood Education: Being Essential

While most schools throughout the world closed for at least several months, if not much longer, some of us stayed open from the very start of the pandemic. My own school, Discovery Village Childcare Center and Preschool, closed for just eight school days at the very end of March 2020. Confusion and fear were rampant at the time. My leadership team and I needed to take a quick breath, assess what was happening around us, and make decisions. During those eight days I reached out far and wide for guidance on health and safety protocols. I engaged in soul searching, unsure as to what was right. What if somebody became ill at my center? How could I afford to stay open with so many families suspending enrollment and stopping their tuition payments? How would I navigate the multiple challenges unfolding unpredictably at breakneck speed?

In those intense early days of the pandemic, the term *hero* was frequently applied to those of us referred to as essential workers, serving in positions that were allowed or even encouraged to continue operating while the rest of the world shut down or went remote. As a result, some heaped effusive praise on me. Still, there were others who judged me a villain for keeping my child care center open when they felt all staff and students should be sheltering in place at home. Some harshly condemned my decisions that contradicted their own opinions. Still others viewed me as a victim, seeing the financial peril faced by small businesses generally and child care centers specifically. I rejected all of these designations. I was neither hero nor villain nor victim. I was merely an ordinary person in extraordinary times, striving to do right by the families and children I serve and the staff I employ. That commitment to doing right offered me my North Star, my guiding light by which I would make the many choices that were to come.

Throughout it all, vision and values I had not even known I held so deeply rose to the surface. In a world of chaos and uncertainty, I wanted to create an environment of calm, a haven of hope. To that end, I made numerous decisions that distinguished my center from many others locally and nationally. Perhaps most significant was allowing parents to enter even as most programs shifted to dropping off and picking up children at the door to limit COVID-19 exposure. I tried at-the-door drop-off and pickup for about a day at the beginning of the pandemic and again for several weeks in January 2021 after we experienced a number of COVID-19 cases. Seeing teary-eyed children and parents saying goodbye outside tore at my heartstrings, and it felt antithetical to the nurturing oasis, the haven of hope I was intentionally designing. While ensuring I included protocols so that I remained in adherence with the regulations of our local health department, I let parents in. They masked, physically distanced from all but their own children, took their temperature, and completed a health check upon entry. They stayed only briefly, typically less than ten minutes. This ensured, based on health department protocols, that even if a parent contracted COVID-19, we would not have to quarantine. With those safety protocols in place, parents entered, creating some feeling of normalcy in a world in which we longed for the normal, the routine, the daily interactions with individuals outside our own households. In addition, having parents enter the center let them experience our health and safety protocols. This was powerful both in keeping us accountable and in reassuring parents.

Relationships among parents and between parents and staff strengthened. Yet our approach was by no means right for everybody. As spring turned to summer and new families enrolled, a small number left, a portion of these with anger. One made a point of blasting us on multiple review sites, dissatisfied with the safety protocols at the center. Current families rose to offer support, privately and publicly, sharing their appreciation and trust in our learning, care, and health and safety protocols. Having experienced the angst of people who were not ready to return, we actively and kindly encouraged people not to enroll if they were too apprehensive or fearful.

As summer turned to fall and then to winter, even amid the ongoing uncertainty and fear, we continued to enroll more students. New Year's Day 2021 was momentous, bittersweet, and highly emotional for me. For months, in serious jeopardy of having to shut my doors permanently, I had focused on the goal of still being open by the beginning of the new year. And here I was, on New Year's Day, not only still in business but celebrating an enrollment that was back to pre-pandemic numbers. My gratitude was genuine yet at the same time mixed with unnerving dread about what might be coming. There was growing concern both locally and nationally about a likely winter spike in COVID-19 cases.

For the previous ten months of the pandemic, my center had escaped the shutdowns and COVID-19 scares many had experienced. One of our team members had become ill with what was almost certainly COVID-19 in April 2020, during the very early days of the pandemic. With extremely limited testing available and hospitals overwhelmed, she was told to just stay home for at least fourteen days and until symptom-free. The telemedicine doctor with whom she spoke instructed her to go to an emergency room only if she found herself unable to breathe. With news of this almost certain, albeit untested case of COVID-19, the center closed for just one day for cleaning and disinfecting. Nobody was required to quarantine.

By January 2021 the landscape was entirely different. COVID-19 testing was readily available, and contact tracing called for a ten-day quarantine for anybody who came in close contact with an individual who tested positive for COVID-19. I told my director, assistant director, and educational coordinator to be ready for anything. Perhaps there would be required shutdowns. If not, families might choose to shelter in place. Minimally, I imagined we would experience COVID-19 exposures and positive COVID-19 cases at the center and have to come in and out of quarantine.

Throughout January and February, we were hit with case after case of COVID-19—teachers, parents, and even children. I was consumed with fear for the safety of those at my center. Thankfully, all who contracted COVID-19 fully recovered. Not knowing that would be the case, I felt myself constantly tense and fearful. Each morning, I offered a silent prayer, hoping to make it through the day without somebody calling to tell me of a COVID-19 exposure or positive COVID-19 test. Too often, those prayers went unanswered as the dreaded calls kept coming.

I committed to transparency and accessibility, immediately passing all the information I had about COVID-19 exposures, positive cases, and quarantines to families and staff. I gave my cell phone number to the entire school community, letting them know I was accessible anytime, including evenings and weekends. A few families temporarily suspended enrollment, feeling it safer to care for their children at home. A few left the center permanently. Twice, an anonymous report to the New York State Office of Children and Family Services, my licensing agency, claimed I had not appropriately followed the Department of Health protocols for reporting COVID-19 cases. Once the local Department of Health received an anonymous complaint. Both my licensor at the Office of Children and Family Services and the Department of Health quickly deemed the complaints unfounded. Despite those few cases of trepidation and suspicion, the majority of families showered us with appreciation and gratitude. Most not only remained at Discovery Village but grew even closer to one another and to the center. They coordinated meetings of a new parent and teacher community group, connecting on video calls and through a messaging app. They scheduled physically distanced meetups outdoors at local parks and forged new friendships.

Enrollment grew far faster than we ever anticipated. By spring of 2021, with a rapidly expanding wait list, we could not find staff to meet increasing enrollment demands. Child care centers and many other businesses throughout the country were experiencing similar unprecedented staffing shortages. Having just experienced massive unemployment, we had not anticipated this challenge and found ourselves again seeking ways to adapt as rapidly as possible. With just under 100 students and a wait list of more than 60, we technically had some spots available, as we were not yet at our licensed capacity of 128 students. Yet one of our classrooms remained closed and several more were intentionally not at capacity.

For weeks, short-staffed, I spent mornings in a toddler classroom and afternoons in an infant classroom. I then spent evenings doing much of the work that I could not get to during the day as I was covering classes. The rest of my leadership team were doing the same. We were exhausted.

Still, it wasn't enough. We had to close several days when we did not have the staff to keep the center open because of ongoing staffing shortages. For months we reduced our hours, closing at five o'clock instead of six. Yet even with these challenges, fewer than a handful of families left, and our wait list kept growing, reaching to well over 150 by the final months of 2021. Families showed tremendous support and appreciation for all we were doing, and together we faced this newest obstacle with creativity and resilience, skills we had much practice with during the previous months. We had set a tone of calm, living into our vision and our values, finding ways to improve the quality of learning and care we offered with each and every new obstacle. Similar experiences were happening at early childhood centers throughout the country and the world.

Hope Day School and Tomorrow's Promise, both in Texas, are exemplars of the inspirational successes of those in early childhood who led the way for others, remaining open from the very start.

Hope and Promise

When COVID hit, executive director Cori Berg at Hope Day School knew her faith-based child care center had to remain open. Located near the medical district in Dallas, Texas, Cori took very seriously her center's role as a critical service, supporting the children of essential workers. Yet not everyone embraced Cori's work. Many felt that child care centers should be closed so teachers and children could quarantine. Feeling abandoned and alone, Cori set off on two deeply connected journeys, one individually as a professional and the other as the leader of Hope Day School.

Seeking a network of support, Cori reached out to colleagues. She began hosting live discussions on social media. Her earliest conversations focused on the many demands facing child care centers, including health and safety protocols as well as challenging financial decisions. From there, Cori became a voice of care and meaning in the greater early childhood educator community. She guided colleagues in accessing the emotional side of leadership, something she recognized as a gap in many early childhood education leadership training courses. Cori's programming encompassed topics including fear, self-care, finding joy, and compassion.

"Educators need to know other people are having similar struggles," Cori asserted. During the hard moments, "you start to feel really bad and search for answers." She was in that position herself and found that even before the pandemic, most available training programs didn't go deep enough. During the pandemic, the problem was exacerbated. When leaders had to make imperfect decisions, they struggled, overwhelmed with exhaustion and self-doubt.

Even before the pandemic, Hope Day School had been short-staffed, with an unfilled leadership position. "When COVID hit we had triple the work, and we already had only two people doing the work of three." Cori hadn't taken a single vacation day in two years, and the exhaustion was overwhelming. One day, Cori let her assistant director know she was taking the day off. Hearing the anxiety in her assistant director's response, Cori lovingly changed course and promised to come in. This decision prompted her assistant director to change her mind and plead with Cori to take the day. As Cori remembered, "It was a pivotal moment in which we felt how we care so much about each other that we forget about self-care." The pair committed to making it OK for each other to take days off, in the process intentionally focusing on "teaching teachers that management is human."

Even with renewed commitment to self-care, the most challenging conversations for Cori continued to be conveying her own needs to those closest to her. While being present for her community, Cori has often felt alone. For example, she remembers the day she was rushing to complete her loan application for the federal Paycheck Protection Program. Like many small businesses and nonprofits throughout the country, Cori had been passed over when funding in round one of the loan program ran out. Receiving the loan could mean the difference between surviving or having to close the doors permanently. This high-stakes task was out of her comfort zone, and her stress was substantial. As Cori hurried to get to the accountant, one of her teachers approached her. Upset, the teacher asked why Cori was not doing daily mental health check-ins with each of the teachers. At that moment, Cori realized her teachers truly did not understand how much it was taking from her to pay the bills and keep the school from permanently closing. She has since focused on ways of sensitively and honestly conveying that larger picture to her staff.

As a creative and open thinker, throughout the pandemic Cori looked for ways not only to navigate through as safely and compassionately as possible but also to deepen the quality of learning in her school. She embraced the Waldorf approach, weaving its holistic perspectives into Hope Day School's grounding in spirituality and Christian heritage. The infusion of what Cori calls "Craft with a big C" has been powerful. "This includes skill with our hands and musical instruments, the arts, storytelling, fables, and imagination. It connects with me as a person and with us as a school," she reflected.

In many ways, Hope Day School had been well poised to navigate adversity. Resilience and openness had already been part of the very fabric of the community. For the first sixty-five years of the school's existence, Hope Day School was housed in a Methodist church. Then, three years prior to the pandemic, a new pastor came to the church. She shifted the institution's mission, and the school found it needed to secure a new space quickly. A father of one of the students was the senior minister at Cathedral of Hope, which serves a predominantly LGBTQ community. He offered space in its large church, located nearby, and the school moved. Hope Day School's community is not primarily LGBTQ, so the process of culturally integrating with the church was an experience of learning and growth. Embarking on this integration set a foundation of openness and a willingness to stretch beyond the known.

Even with a solid foundation, the demands of navigating through the pandemic challenged Hope Day School to its core. "The hardest part for teachers, as for me, is that there was no training for this. Some teachers were too afraid in the beginning. Some were too high risk. Some were not a match and couldn't do it. They didn't trust the process enough. I couldn't build it fast enough," Cori said.

"During the most challenging moments, it was easy to want to blame somebody, anybody: our licensing agencies or the CDC for giving incomplete and imperfect guidance and most definitely our programs' leadership," Cori said. She absorbed her share of painful blame for some of the difficult choices she had to make. For example, she decided it was important to have smaller groups of children with only one teacher to minimize possible exposure to the virus. Previously, she'd had a coteaching model with two teachers working together in each classroom. Additionally, Cori decided that due to low enrollment she would combine three- and four-year-olds into one classroom. Each of these decisions, among others, sparked upset for a small number of teachers. Anytime a staff member resigned, Cori reflected on whether there was anything she could have done better, remaining ever open to learning while acknowledging that there are always things out of her control.

Through it all, Cori emerged as a voice for hope and resilience both in her school and in the broader field. Creativity and commitment among her staff, colleagues, and families was high, but so was stress, anxiety, and even trauma. "Teachers and administrators that made it through the pandemic are pretty special people," she shared with palpable emotion. "They have resilience, tolerance for imperfection, and the ability to give grace to other people." The pandemic, for Cori, has been a time of deep self-reflection, of finding that it is through adversity that we grow our wings. Through everything, she has focused on finding joy. "Joy," said Cori, "is my philosophy of child care."

The Calm in the Eye of the Storm

Tomorrow's Promise, The Montessori School of Huntsville, Texas, played a unique role during the pandemic. The county where the school is located is home to seven prisons with more than twenty thousand inmates, including the Texas State Penitentiary at Huntsville. Eighty percent of parents with children enrolled at the center are essential workers, including EMS personnel, firefighters, police officers, and nurses. But the vast majority serve as correctional officers. While many other parents throughout the country feared sending their children to child care, a substantial majority of families in Huntsville were more fearful about what would happen if their center closed. They needed providers who would continue to care for their children even though they themselves were regularly exposed to COVID-19 through their job. Director Kaye Boehning was immediately ready to serve.

Kaye had opened the center, a nonprofit Christian Montessori school, twenty-three years prior to the beginning of the pandemic and had served as director from the very start. Kaye's assistant director had been at the school for twenty-one years. During those many years of serving their relatively small community, Kaye had built a reputation for remaining open for her families despite all obstacles. Neither hurricanes nor ice storms had ever stopped Tomorrow's Promise.

When the pandemic hit, Kaye believed that she had arrived in a particular place at a particular time to solve a particular problem. This did not mean she was not afraid. Kaye connected to her faith to find the courage she needed to move forward. "The first thing I put up by our time clock, the day the pandemic hit, was a quote. 'It takes the same energy to worry as to pray. One leads to panic. The other leads to peace.' I see it as I clock in and clock out. Everybody sees. It is what kept me from panicking."

Kaye quickly focused on cultivating and nurturing an environment in which every child, parent, and staff member would feel truly cared for. "A core group stayed and worked as a team. Everybody stepped up to the plate," Kaye recalled. The experience "cemented us as a family." Kaye could often see the fear and pain in parents' eyes. She remembered one conversation with a single father who serves as a correctional officer. When she asked how he was doing, he couldn't answer. Kaye recognized he was frightened. If he shared how hard it was to be working with inmates with COVID-19, Kaye might say that because of his exposure to COVID-19 he could not bring his child to school. She reassured the father: "It's OK. We will watch your child."

Throughout it all, Kaye catapulted forward. She put a range of systems in place to improve operations in her school and even expanded her program, opening another building and then purchasing another site, doubling her capacity at the same time many other programs were shutting their doors.

Kaye deliberately nurtured an environment of calm, designing her school as a haven of hope. Children entered each day to see the same caring faces and engage in mostly the same activities, albeit with modified safety protocols. At times, Kaye knew that staff members were afraid. Yet she modeled calmness. "It was hard for me," she said. "I was scared to death and telling everyone it would be OK." Still, through it all, Tomorrow's Promise remained open, a vitally essential service providing for vitally essential workers.

In the rapidly changing landscape in which we found ourselves, just as I sat to write this section about Hope Day School and Tomorrow's Promise in February 2021, news came of more crisis in Texas. With extreme wintry weather, the state's power grid failed, leaving much of the state without power. Loss of heat was soon followed by disruptions to the water supply, leaving millions without drinkable water.

I saw a despairing social media post from Kaye, sharing that she had to close for the first time in her school's history. The rolling blackouts meant it was almost certain her center would be without heat in freezing temperatures. I reached out to both Cori and Kaye and was brought back to the intensity of the early days of the pandemic. That sensation was widespread. Kaye said that in Texas, many were calling the storm "Snowvid." Cori described a sense of reliving the stress and fear of the earliest days of the pandemic. Most of both Cori's and Kaye's staff members and families had no power. Kaye shared how her heart broke hearing parents reach out hoping the school was open, desperately wanting a place where their children could get warm. She anticipated many COVID-19 cases, as people had done what they could to keep warm, huddling together with extended family and friends. Cori had similar emotions. Most staff in her community were afraid to go to warming centers, as they'd heard that many people there were not wearing masks.

When people ventured out, the supermarket shelves were bare. With the disruption to the water supply, people were boiling snow. Both Cori and Kaye were under immense stress, wanting to help and not knowing what to do. They reopened as soon as they were able, remaining present as best they could for their families and staff. Looking ahead to the possibility—or probability—of future disasters, Kaye and her husband decided that when this storm ended, they would invest in a full-building generator for their school. They wanted to be open and able to serve.

3

Outdoor Learning Programs: Actively Reimagining Possibilities

Many early childhood programs closed briefly and then reopened fully or primarily outdoors. The shift to fully outdoor learning was not simple, but as the virus was less transmissible outside, it was urgent. Yet safety was not the only motivation. Many educators and families were giving ever more attention to connecting to nature and caring for our planet.

Discovery Child Care Centre in Barrie, Ontario, Canada; Beacon Hebrew Alliance Preschool in Beacon, New York; and Building Blocks Preschool in Highland, Michigan, closed briefly. When they reopened, they did so with a deepened commitment to outdoor learning, long core to their approaches while experiencing a renewed energy and sense of possibility. Kaleidoscope Community School in Salem, Oregon, and Muck and Wonder Farm School in Sacramento, California, both recommitted to outdoor learning and extended their offerings to serve school-age children.

Living into Our Values

"For me, it is a choice every day to see this time as an opportunity," said Jessica Holder, pedagogical leader at Discovery Child Care Centre, a forest and nature school. Along with director and owner Karen Eilersen, Jessica made the deliberate choice to use the months COVID forced school closure to improve.

Mandated to close from March 17, 2020, until the middle of June, along with all other child care programs in Ontario, Karen and Jessica spent the time in deliberate introspection and planning. With lots of conversation in Canada and throughout the world about the need for child care programs to open so parents could get back to work, Karen aspired for more. "I didn't want to open if we couldn't live into our values. We are not about warehousing children," Karen said.

As part of their extensive exploration into living their values, Karen and Jessica participated in a webinar I offered in June 2020. Titled *Havens of Hope*, the webinar presented for the first time the ideas that have been expanded into this book. Listening to the notion of educational approaches born out of crisis, Karen was reminded of the founding of Discovery Child Care Centre in 1998. With a dearth of available indoor spaces for child care centers, families in Ontario were struggling to access quality care for their children. Some expressed interest in outdoor learning. Karen stood as a pioneer when she opened the center. At the nature-based preschool, children spend all day outside except lunch and naptime. The emergent program builds learning experiences from children's interests. Teachers document the learning journey for the purpose of evaluating, reflecting, and sharing with families. They embrace natural materials and loose parts, encouraging creative and imaginative play.

When child care centers in Canada were allowed to reopen in June, Karen and Jessica chose to pause for just a bit longer. "We made the pedagogic decision to slow down. We decided to dedicate time with our educators, exploring how we want to create livable futures for our children," Karen said.

Remaining closed through the summer was by no means an obvious choice. Discovery Child Care Centre had been well poised to reopen. Discourse in Ontario, as in much of the world, focused on how to get children outside where the virus does not spread as easily. Additionally, after twenty-two years leading the school, Karen had developed excellent rapport and trust with her families. Confident that she could have had full enrollment immediately, Karen believed that the enormity of what was happening in the world was opening new educational possibilities. Never before could the entire faculty at this full-time, full-year program come together for a month of professional learning and planning.

"How can we dream through this time?" Jessica asked the school's faculty when they returned in August. "What programs and what spaces do we want to create?" Together educators carefully peeled back the layers on what was working at their school and what was not. They set out to reconceptualize their entire program, looking at everything: policies, strategies, approaches, physical space usage, and more.

Delving into insights from a range of thought leaders, most particularly Brené Brown and Simon Sinek, Jessica and Karen led teachers in exploring a wide variety of topics through the lens of early childhood. Emphasizing mental health, they considered topics such as fear, how learning happens, and what learning can be when the appropriate conditions are met. They focused on ensuring that faculty not only felt safe but also felt confident they could live their values and do their job well in the midst of the pandemic.

Discovery Child Care Centre reopened in September 2020 at half capacity with double the staff. Karen made a deliberate choice not to open at full capacity immediately. She wanted to take time to actualize their deepened vision. This decision was made financially possible because during the pandemic the governments of Ontario and Canada provided subsidies of up to 75 percent of staff wages.

Karen and Jessica connect their values-driven approach to their roots as a forest and nature school. They are also inspired by the way Reggio-inspired learning is grounded in standing strong against oppression, injustice, and inequity. At Discovery Child Care Centre, there is an unapologetic focus on the political, in the broadest and deepest sense of the word. Questions posed at Discovery Child Care Centre include *What is the issue early education is responding to at this time?* and *What does that mean for our practice?* During the months of the pandemic, they increased focus on the environment and sustainability.

With the new year came new challenges. An outbreak of a COVID-19 variant in a local long-term care home resulted in yet another lockdown. In addition, more stringent health mandates were implemented, requiring staff to remain home if they had any symptoms, including a runny nose. Quarantine requirements changed so that if anybody in a household had to quarantine, the entire household had to quarantine. The center struggled to have sufficient staff to remain open on some days.

Still Jessica and her team persevered. Amid the heaviness of the outside world, Discovery felt like a haven of hope. Jessica reported that staff were saying the center was the place they felt the safest, where they could be themselves and live their values. "Many of our staff say this is almost a reprieve, almost an escape from the rest of the world. That is very meaningful," she said.

For Discovery Child Care Centre, living into their values also means behaving in ways they view as ethical. They have long been grounded in a passion for sustainability and recycling and are extremely intentional about materials they bring into the program. They are additionally transitioning to a fully plant-based diet for the children: whole grains, fresh fruits and vegetables, and whole foods, with no processed food and no meat, fish, or dairy. The decision is focused both on their commitment to sustainability as well as their grounding in health and wellness.

"COVID shifted and changed us all," Karen said. Committed to ensuring that the momentum continues, she and Jessica remain intentional about their leadership choices, determined to support their team in continuing to thrive.

When the Impossible Suddenly Seemed Possible

"The impossible suddenly seemed possible," reflected Ilana Friedman, director and lead teacher of the Beacon Hebrew Alliance Preschool. The pandemic forced dramatic change at this small synagogue preschool, located in New York's Hudson Valley. Ilana and her community drew strength from the emphasis the school has long placed on relationships, community, and social-emotional learning. She was invigorated by the ways her community sustained connections during what could easily have been a time of great social isolation. She committed to finding new ways to serve.

Ilana had become the preschool's founding director five years prior to the pandemic. She came to the position after teaching elementary students for many years. Her choice to transition to early childhood education was both professional and personal. With a toddler-aged child of her own, Ilana had become deeply engaged in inquiry and play for younger children. The opportunity to design an early childhood program in her very own community was compelling.

Beacon Hebrew Alliance Preschool began with six children in one classroom. Ilana designed a magical experience, grounded in exploration and wonder. Children tended their very own garden every day with guidance from Ilana's assistant, a flower farmer who brought a passion for gardening to the school. Filled with art materials and glow lights, the classroom invited curiosity. Ilana carefully crafted learning that emerged from children's interests. In time, the school grew to serve fourteen children with three teachers.

When the pandemic hit, Beacon Hebrew Alliance Preschool shifted to remote learning, but this did not mean that all learning would be online. Ilana sent home a kit with materials tailored to hands-on learning, including cards featuring yoga poses telling the story of Passover. She also sent each child materials to fill a lavender sachet, inviting families to create a peace corner at home. The home peace corners mirrored the peace corner children loved in their classroom. Perhaps most significantly, Ilana deliberately included materials that invited children to spend time outdoors. She gave them seed packets for spring vegetable gardening. She also designed a multidisciplinary learning unit about birds and sent home materials each family could use to engage in an investigation about birds. Not wanting children to spend lots of time on a screen, Ilana was intentional about the type and amount of screen-based learning options she offered.

On the last day of the 2019–2020 academic school year, in June 2020, Ilana hosted a video-conference ceremony for families. In preparation, children made beeswax candles, created art for an art show, and visited the school garden to decorate pots and plant mint. The online ceremony engaged the senses, replete with lavender sachets, candlelit photographs of artwork, songs, movement, and dramatic play. Initially Ilana had believed remote learning was the antithesis of meaningful preschool education. Yet she ended the year feeling hopeful.

Proud of how her school had adapted to a remote learning environment, Ilana and her community nonetheless longed to return to in-person learning. The school would reopen in the fall as a 100 percent outdoor program. Ilana spent the summer researching forest and nature-based preschools around the world. She set up the infrastructure for rain fly tarps and tents to give shelter from the weather. Parents installed a laundry sink outdoors for hand washing. A neighbor with skill in carpentry built a privy to shelter portable potties for

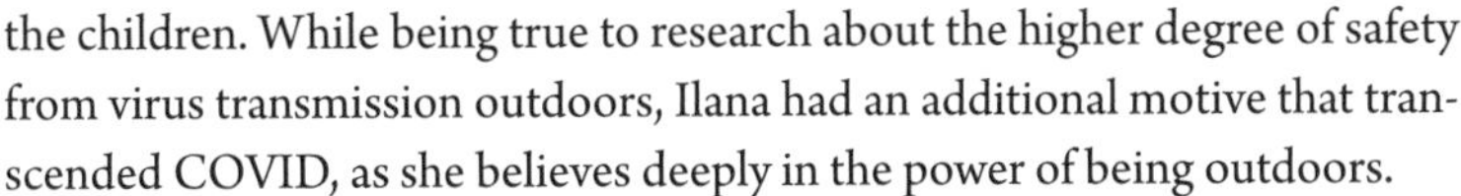

the children. While being true to research about the higher degree of safety from virus transmission outdoors, Ilana had an additional motive that transcended COVID, as she believes deeply in the power of being outdoors.

Beacon Hebrew Alliance Preschool reopened running four days a week for just under three hours a day. Operating an entirely outdoor program was a big change. Ilana was sensitive to parents' uncertainty, both about COVID and about the weather. She allowed parents to enroll trimester by trimester, rather than for the entire year. Very quickly, uncertainty shifted to gratitude. Ilana witnessed a demonstrable reduction of stress for parents and children alike. The school became a regular community for students and families during times of isolation. For some, it served an even more powerful role as a refuge from the world's chaos.

There were fears other than pandemic. Running a Jewish preschool fully outdoors in an area with a white supremacist presence, Ilana and her community took precautions, including forming a security committee. January 6, 2021, when protesters attacked the US Capitol in Washington, DC, was particularly frightening for the preschool. They remained in close contact with local security and were proud to be able to carry on, even in the face of fear.

Operating a fully outdoor preschool requires significant adaptability. "Just when you think you know what the next day's plan is, the weather changes. You have to stay flexible," Ilana explained. Perhaps the most significant realization for her was that everything can be learned outdoors. Prior to the pandemic, the school had embraced a deep connection to nature. Children tended to their garden daily and enjoyed recess and social-emotional and gross-motor learning experiences outdoors, but the more academic parts of their program had happened indoors. During COVID Ilana found ways to use the outdoor space as a full-fledged classroom.

Ilana delighted in how connected the children became to the small woody area on their grounds, their garden, and the chickens living in their neighbor's yard. She watched in amazement as children observed the outdoors, attentive to trees or digging layers in the soil to explore the composition of the earth. Through sustained time outdoors, children gained a deeper sense of oneness with natural elements in their outdoor space.

The Beacon Hebrew Alliance Preschool community had always been tight-knit, but the experience of moving online and then moving outside strengthened family engagement. A supportive spirit and tremendous generosity permeated the preschool, increasing the sense of interdependence between staff and families. "By working together we were able to give children the opportunity to learn in community," Ilana relayed.

While at times Ilana missed her cozy indoor classroom with the felt board, library, and light table with sprouting seeds, she became an even stronger advocate for outdoor learning than she had been pre-pandemic. "Working outdoors all the time feels like we are exercising all of ourselves," Ilana shared.

A Place of Awe and Wonder

Building Blocks Preschool is, in the words of owner Suzanne Gabli, "a place of awe and wonder." Set on two and a half acres of its own land, the school backs up onto another five thousand acres of state land in Highland, Michigan. The magnificent setting, which has long been integral to Building Blocks' nature-based approach, became vital during the pandemic.

The school closed for just over three months at the beginning of the pandemic, although Suzanne worked more intensely and longer hours than ever before. Her efforts were threefold, focusing on (1) keeping children and families connected and engaged, (2) drafting COVID-19 health and safety protocols, and (3) preparing for reopening. Throughout it all, Suzanne guided her faculty to remain grounded in Building Blocks' vision for quality learning and care. Faculty scheduled home visits with each of the children, wearing masks, remaining six feet apart from students and their families, and delivering activity boxes. Suzanne scheduled a weekly video conference lunch bunch so children could connect with her and with each other. Rather than holding the school's Light at Night Halloween party on site, she encouraged families to create their own light at night displays at home and share pictures with the community.

When the school reopened immediately after July 4, 2020, Suzanne immersed herself in planning quality learning at an even higher level than pre-COVID. She strengthened her play-based vision for learning and encouraged her faculty to slow down and allow children to set their own pace, documenting learning through portfolio assessments. Suzanne said she and her faculty found letting go of tight control to be "very freeing. Once you feel free, the children feel free. They will feel the energy you bring to the day."

Children spent approximately 70 percent of their day outdoors, staying inside all day for only four brutally cold days during the winter. Building Blocks' outdoor learning areas included places for math manipulatives; art activities; play with open-ended loose parts; gardens, including butterfly gardens; a mud kitchen; and a stage. A teacher with a passion for literacy created a story walk, with storybooks in outdoor brochure boxes. "Schools shut down and child care didn't. Society was saying 'everything stops,' and child care was saying, 'Let's go,'" Suzanne relayed. "We armored up and we carried on during the pandemic. We didn't know in those first three months what it would look like. This happened by holding onto joy, a sense of routines, and a foundation in our core strengths."

Through it all, Suzanne dug into her faith, leading intentionally from a place of love and not fear. She relayed that the Bible says not to fear 365 times, and she found comfort in those passages. While more than four hundred child care programs in Michigan closed, Building Blocks got better. The transformation at Building Blocks has been powerful, but it wasn't easy. Suzanne describes it as a rebuilding, brick by brick. She believes educators can choose which bricks they pull from the rubble: control and scarcity or love and abundance. She is so very proud that her teachers have embraced love and abundance.

A Journey of Change and Growth

Kaleidoscope Community School in Salem, Oregon, has always been deeply grounded both in the Reggio-inspired approach and the philosophy and principles of the Unitarian Universalist Church in which the school is housed. Kaleidoscope is the realization of founder Ashley Acers's dream. Ashley had spent her entire career in early childhood education, serving as a teacher, director, and program director before spending twelve years codesigning, building, and selling schools. Then she traveled to Reggio Emilia, Italy, in 2017, and the quality of learning she experienced there was beyond what she previously imagined possible. She returned to the United States determined to bring quality Reggio-inspired learning back with her. On July 17, 2017, shortly after her return from Italy, Ashley was sitting outside at her church when her pastor walked by. She asked whether he had ever thought about opening a preschool. Without missing a beat, her pastor told her that she would be the perfect person to do so. That very September, just a month and a half later, Ashley opened Kaleidoscope Community School. Ashley hired Molly Brown as director. Within several years, Ashley and Molly grew the preschool to full capacity with a wait list.

In 2019, Kaleidoscope Community School embarked on a journey of change and growth. It leased a five-acre pasture next door to the school, including forest area and open space. Ashley and Molly filled the pasture with roosters, bunnies, and their very own one-hundred-pound pig. In that wonderland, children climbed trees, ran through meadows, dug in the dirt, and cared for the animals. Their emergent curriculum, stemming directly from children's interests, moved quite naturally from an emphasis on art to a focus on playful investigations in nature. Ashley and Molly next embarked on the process of becoming an accredited elementary school using the Global Village distance-learning curriculum, which integrates self-knowledge, social justice, and sustainability studies with the core subjects.

Then the pandemic hit, dramatically accelerating Kaleidoscope's journey. When the local public schools announced they would not be resuming in-person learning until January 2021, interest in Kaleidoscope's new elementary school program grew. Kaleidoscope prepared to welcome twelve preschoolers, fifteen kindergartners, and fifteen children in first through third grade who would learn in mixed-age groupings. Eight staff members would serve the group of forty-two pioneering students.

On what would have been the first day of the 2020–2021 school year, forest fires blazed. Two weeks passed before it was safe to open. Later that winter, an ice storm and burst water main forced the school to briefly close again. With the direct experience of such extreme weather, children became interested in tracking weather patterns and finding ways to care for the planet. They got outside every day, noticing small and large changes in weather and exploring the natural world.

Ashley and Molly ordered three large outdoor yurts to serve as the primary learning space for a pod of ten to twelve children. Excitement grew as one of the yurts arrived via air freight, with two more in transit by boat. Disaster struck as the first yurt awaited installation. Somebody stole the trailers with the parts inside. Devastated by the news, Ashley and Molly had to tell the children that their school had been stolen.

News of the stolen yurt spread widely. Inmates at the Oregon State Penitentiary heard a broadcast about the stolen yurt and organized a fundraiser. Receiving support from the inmates was a profound experience for the children. At Kaleidoscope they often talk about how everyone has a story. When inmates stood up as the very first people to lend assistance, children's

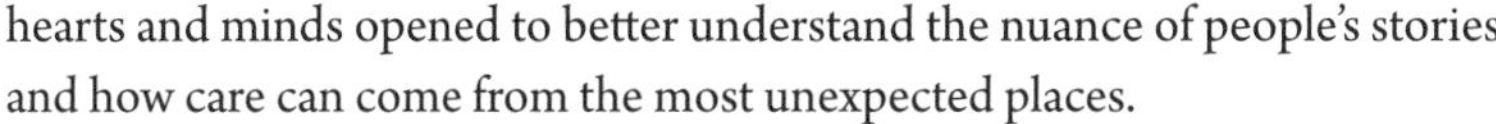

hearts and minds opened to better understand the nuance of people's stories and how care can come from the most unexpected places.

Many other challenges existed, with finances high on the list. For many months the school could operate at only half of its licensed capacity due to local requirements placed on child care centers that remained open during the early months of the pandemic. Costs were much more than income coming in. So Ashley rented out her own house and temporarily moved into one of the yurts, using the rental money to pay off the loan for the structures. And Dotty the pig moved in with her! They've made it all work. "The universe keeps rising so we can keep walking," Ashley asserted. Reflecting on her journey, she smiled and, with a twinkle in her eye, said, "We got a pig, and it all went from there."

A Wonderland of Playful Possibilities

Muck and Wonder Farm School, previously a nature-based parent cooperative preschool, is a wonderland of playful possibilities. Located in Sacramento, California, in a large schoolhouse built in 1949, Muck and Wonder opened in 2018. The school is an arm of Waking the Village, a nonprofit organization that supports youth in overcoming homelessness. All proceeds from Muck and Wonder are used to fund the vital work of Waking the Village.

Before the pandemic, Muck and Wonder created a farm experience designed to engage preschool children and their grown-ups in a combination of real-life contribution and play. Parents or caregivers attended with their children. Preschoolers took an active role in caring for the goats, pigs, and chickens living on the school's grounds. They baked their own bread, prepared healthy meals, and washed their own dishes. Using real tools, the preschoolers put together much of the school's furniture. Outside, a zip line and an old car stand in place of a more traditional playground, providing a vintage feel to the imaginative play and exploration.

When the pandemic hit, Muck and Wonder temporarily closed its doors. Director Jenna Maggard used those several months to plan adaptations to serve families safely and effectively. Local public schools had shifted entirely to remote learning, and many families were searching for child care along with community for their children. Many were seeking outdoor pods in parks or nature reserves because of indications that the virus did not spread as easily outdoors. Licensed to serve preschool, Jenna applied to her state's licensing agency for a waiver to serve elementary school children.

Muck and Wonder reopened in June 2020 as a full-day program for elementary school children, supplementing work they would do online while enrolled in their own schools. Jenna put COVID safety protocols in place and extended the school day so that Muck and Wonder would be open Monday to Friday from 8:30 a.m. until 4 p.m., meeting the child care needs of families with school-age children. "This year has been about serving in the way we need to serve. All other plans are on the back burner," Jenna stated.

Children spend the majority of their time outdoors learning, exploring, and helping on the farm. They also spend time in a co-learning cafe Jenna designed. Mirroring coworking spaces for adults, children have work spaces with laptops and headphones where they can attend their school's remote classes and complete assignments.

The hardest modification for Jenna was the shift from a cooperative, attended jointly by preschool children and their grown-ups, to a program serving children alone. She longs to find a way to more seamlessly include children in the world of adults. Rather than shuffling children off to their own worlds, Jenna imagines a village-like environment in which children are woven into the work of community while still engaging in the heart of play. She wonders how children could be with families more and in school and child care less. That being said, Jenna sees the benefit of school, specifically schools offering a mixed-age setting and emphasizing trusting relationships, real-world skills, and child-directed play. These core ideals have stood at the heart of Muck and Wonder, both when it served as a preschool cooperative and when it transformed into a farm school supporting remote learning.

4

Going Remote: Staying Connected While Physically Apart

In the early weeks of the pandemic, as people spoke of remote learning in early childhood, I could not wrap my mind around what that might be. How could young children, who need nurturing, supervision, and tremendous engagement, connect remotely? It sounded ridiculous. Yet, committed to serving, we quickly figured it out.

As financial worry gripped me, I briefly considered creating an online preschool program for which I would charge. Ultimately, I decided against it, choosing instead to focus my energies on strengthening my core program. However, I did want to offer value to families who were suspending enrollment. To that end, my teachers and I created free virtual learning experiences, welcoming children and families at home into the classroom.

Other programs invested far more in remote learning experiences than we did at Discovery Village, in the process expanding views of what early childhood learning can be. Some educators who excelled in this work include

Josiane Sawaya at the Santa Clara Unified School District in California, Nelum Walpola at White Dove Montessori in Texas, Karina Wyllie at Koala Park Daycare in my own Westchester County, New York, and Joy Anderson, who leads a large group of preschool owners through her membership-based community, Preschool System and Preschool All Stars Membership. Susan MacDonald of Inspiring New Perspectives found ways to support many early childhood educators through remote professional learning. Each of these extraordinary educators brought unique perspectives on what is core to learning and care, whether remote or in person.

Parent-Participation, Play-Based Learning

Josiane Sawaya's parent-participation, play-based preschool is part of the Santa Clara Unified School District in California. Categorized as part of the district's adult education program, the preschool is unlike most in that the registered student is a parent or other grown-up, not the child. Children attend Monday, Wednesday, and Friday mornings, and the registered grown-up attends once a week. The hope is that parents can coordinate their work schedules for the once-a-week commitment.

At the school, children and grown-ups begin the day learning together. They participate in a full-class circle time, as well as hands-on learning activities in small groups. After snack the children go outside to play with the assistant teacher and half of the grown-ups. The other half of the grown-ups learn parenting skills, early childhood development, and early childhood education with Josiane. "No matter how strong an educational program is, if parents are not partnering and not empowered with knowledge to partner, there will be imbalance," she explained. Supporting parents, many of whom are immigrants like Josiane herself, has long been a significant part of her work. During the pandemic, her work with parents became even more meaningful to her, sparking new goals and new professional possibilities.

Josiane was born and raised in Lebanon, and her childhood and teenage years were marked by numerous wars, lasting from the 1970s to the early 1990s. As a result, Josiane knows fear. She also knows hope and resilience. Spending weeks at a time throughout her childhood years in bunkers without windows, Josiane found strength and comfort in her mother's calm courage as she filled her children's ears and hearts with conversation about the future, planning activities for when they could leave the bunker. "Now I understand her need for hope," Josiane shared. She spent the months of the pandemic actively following her mother's example, bringing hope and normalcy to her husband and four children as well as the students and families enrolled in her school.

"I was so scared, and I was thinking about my students and their parents also feeling scared," Josiane said. When her school fully shut down, she committed to connecting with her students and their families in any way she safely could. Friday had been their last day of school prior to quarantine, and by Monday, Josiane had invited families in her class to participate in a videoconference circle time. "I don't know how I did it. It was the most chaotic circle time," she said.

Josiane's online teaching improved dramatically over time. She and her coteacher together developed an engaging remote learning program. They followed students' interests, tailoring the program to focus more on science and cooking, two interests that many of the students shared.

Throughout the time learning online, Josiane redefined what a field trip can be. She brought students outside to her own garden via video conference, getting students interested in gardening and vegetables. She virtually brought students into her living room, which her eight-year-old daughter had transformed into a princess tent. The students loved it as her daughter read to them from the tent. "It was a win-win," Josiane shared. Her daughter had been below grade level in reading. With the appreciative audience, her daughter began to enjoy reading, and her skills improved dramatically. Josiane also offered outdoor, socially distanced games on her front lawn for her students and for children in her neighborhood. When one of her students could not attend online classes or her front yard activities, she walked to his home to visit him, remaining masked and physically distanced.

Caring for others helped Josiane hold past trauma at bay and also manage present grief. "There has been a lot of sadness, scary moments, anxiety, and inner unsettlement," Josiane said. "People lost people they know, people they love. We learned how to give ourselves time to grieve, time to be sad. Then we found ways to accept support and move forward."

In January, Josiane's mother and grandmother both contracted COVID-19. Her mother's condition was very serious. Her grandmother died. While experiencing her own grief, Josiane gained strength in caring for her students.

"With so much sadness, there were many wonderful things, new connections, new routines, new traditions born in this time," she said. "As much as it was hard, it had its beauty. It was a diamond as much as it was rough with grief and loss. There has been a lot of beauty in this time."

Bringing Good, Compassionate Humans into the World

Bringing good, compassionate humans into the world is Nelum Walpola's purpose and passion. Having led White Dove Montessori out of her home since 1995, Nelum has witnessed the powerful impact the educational experience she offers has for the children in her care. While Nelum's preschoolers thrive academically once leaving her program, it is not the traditional accomplishments such as good grades and financial success that make Nelum the proudest but rather the good her students do in the world. For example, one talented former student has dedicated herself to teaching science and fostering four children. In an essay, she credited Nelum as a mentor who changed the course of her life. These deep, long-term connections with students and families, spanning decades and grounded in mutual admiration and respect, are a testament to the profound relationships at the heart of Nelum's signature educational style. In her words, "We can't do anything till we have respect and love for each other, and then everything is possible. It is magic. Students need to know I care. That is my way of teaching."

An emphasis on intentionally nurturing bonds with every child and every family has been part of the very fabric of White Dove Montessori from the school's inception. After moving to Texas from her native Sri Lanka in 1986, Nelum first taught at a Montessori school in Dallas. A number of families at the center approached her with an idea: they would find her a house in which to open her own school. Those founding families, whose vision and belief in her led to the birth of White Dove Montessori, remain to this day as close to Nelum as family.

Nelum's house is a magnificent blend of a schoolhouse, animal shelter, art studio, and art gallery. The creative, compassionate environment she so lovingly cultivates has resonated deeply with her students throughout the years. Children are encouraged to explore and investigate their own interests. Some of those experiences have set the foundation for lifelong commitments.

Nelum speaks with pride about students who are now veterinarians who had helped her care for wounded animals.

At the beginning of the pandemic, Nelum was scared and unsure of what to do. Her brother suggested she offer students the opportunity to learn via video conferencing as schools throughout the country were doing. Self-described as "non-techy," she said that she amazed herself with how smoothly she was able to transition her program to remote learning while opening her home to several students for in-person learning.

Nelum has made remote learning work for students from the age of four and above, something she could not previously have imagined. There have even been unanticipated benefits. Children from families who had moved away joined her class, including a child attending remotely from India. Nelum accomplished the transition by remaining true to her core, focusing on creating an environment of compassion, a haven of hope.

Digging Deep into a Core of Love

Koala Park Daycare was founded on love. "Our main focus is offering a loving, nurturing environment," shared founder and owner Karina Wyllie. With two locations each serving twelve children, Koala Park prides itself on providing children a home away from home.

Located in downstate New York, very close to my own child care center and preschool, Koala Park is located in what was one of the very first COVID-19 hotspots in the country. In the early days of the pandemic, fear was palpable for families and teachers alike. On March 18, 2020, the week public schools in the state shut down, Karina received a text from her head provider. The caregiver shared the frightening news that her husband had been exposed to COVID-19 at work.

With COVID-19 cases rising exponentially in the county and little information yet available on safety protocols, Karina dug deep into her core of love. Not wanting to put anyone at risk, Karina closed both physical locations. Since she was determined to remain present for children and families, she would begin Koala Park Online. At the time, few could fathom teaching infants and toddlers remotely. Teachers were understandably apprehensive. Karina reassured them and guided teachers to connect online to children with love, just as they would in person.

The beginning online sessions were far from perfect. It was extremely challenging to keep such young children engaged remotely. Yet Karina and her teachers found the way. By playfully experimenting, the Koala Park Daycare team found that the more movement they offered, the better. Karina sought out individuals with expertise in the areas the children most enjoyed and hired them to teach enrichment classes, including dance, exercise with a personal trainer, yoga, and two music classes. One music class was interactive, with music and movement related to themes of interest to the children. The other, taught by a Deaf music teacher, included both singing and sign language.

Beyond online classes, Karina provided families with activities they could enjoy with their children anytime. She sent home weekly lesson plans with science, sensory, and art activities. She also posted a video each day featuring a teacher reading a book. To engage children further, Karina invited them to vote between two books each day to choose the read-aloud. Recognizing that parents had many questions and were very afraid, she coordinated sessions via video conferencing for parents to discuss navigating sheltering in place with young children, including a session with a pediatrician and one with a therapist. Each of the guest speakers shared insights on wellness for children and families during a time of pandemic.

In May, embracing her role as an essential service and having learned more about health and safety protocols, Karina reopened slowly, one center at a time. While a few families did not return, Karina quickly reached capacity with new enrollments. Throughout it all Karina communicated and even over-communicated with families, letting them know her plans and asking questions to understand their needs.

Karina reflected on how she made it through, guided by her values. In Karina's words, she was "walking the talk." "You can say a lot, but your actions show who you really are," Karina said. She focused on being present emotionally even during the months of being physically apart. "Every decision takes you down a different path," she explained. "I wanted to do the right thing and make sure to put families and children first. The business was not the priority. The priority was the safety and well-being of everybody: kids, staff, and parents." Like the love in which she grounds her program, the changes to Karina, her teachers, and her two in-home child care centers are palpable and powerful. In Karina's words, "I came out of it a better person."

Shattering the Norms for Learning

Joy Anderson's story began with an act of strength and resilience twelve years before COVID-19 shook the world. After she had spent eight years as a stay-at-home mom raising three young children, her marriage was dissolving, and she needed to find a way to support her children. Seeking a path forward, Joy prayed and was inspired by the memory of a cooperative parent-run preschool she had participated in. Children rotated between the homes of participating families for several hours each day; not for child care, but rather for socialization and learning. Host families organized activities on the days children were in their care. While Joy thrived in leading activities, other moms found hosting far more challenging. They began asking Joy to host additional days. Many of the mothers in the cooperative would have preferred to pay for their children to participate rather than take turns hosting. Joy realized she could open her very own part-time in-home preschool. The possibility energized her. She could work for several hours each day, rather than having to spend the brutally long days required of at-home child care providers, who take care of children full time. Within thirty days, Joy had her program up and running.

Over the following years, Joy opened more part-time preschools in a variety of spaces, ultimately serving more than one thousand students. But then, after a decade of running her schools, Joy made the decision to sell them so she could turn her attention to what had become a deeply held passion, forged during the difficult days immediately following the end of her marriage. Building on her own phenomenal success, Joy launched Preschool System and Preschool All Stars Membership so she could support other moms in starting their own part-time preschools. "No mom should not be able to provide for her family," Joy asserted.

When news of the pandemic and its potential impact spread in the early months of 2020, Joy helped her membership prepare for what it might mean to operate during a pandemic. Initially, members planned for what they would do if a child in their program contracted COVID-19. Then the shelter-in-place orders began. Following district decisions on closures, each day more and more of the preschools in Joy's membership closed. The initial closures culminated mid-March in a full shutdown of in-person learning throughout the entire nation. Joy was determined to help her members keep operating. Seeing schools that were rapidly shifting to remote learning, even though at the time teaching preschool online was almost unfathomable, Joy imagined what online preschool could be. "I never before knew online preschool could even be a thing," Joy shared.

Joy issued a fourteen-day challenge to her membership. Together, they would each create their own online preschool. With energy and creativity, the group completed the ambitious challenge in a mere seven days. The first couple of weeks of online preschool were awkward. Yet, very quickly, schools, families, and children acclimated. The two and a half hours of in-person learning that the preschools had provided was too long for online sessions. Instead, the preschool owners offered two experiences daily, Preschool Pals and Teaching Time. Preschool Pals lasted for thirty minutes each day and included real-time singing, dancing, circle time, and activities promoting social interaction among the preschoolers. Teaching Time featured a prerecorded video of typical preschool learning activities.

Helping preschools move to remote learning renewed Joy's already abundant energy and commitment. She expanded her program, offering support to even more mothers seeking to open either in-person or online preschools. As of the winter of 2021, Joy had helped launch more than five thousand preschools, some in physical locations and others online.

The online option, once unimaginable, became a viable choice that, in Joy's words, "leveled the playing field" for moms. Even moms without access to an appropriate physical location could now open a preschool. "All you need is a computer, internet access, and perhaps a background wall with some preschool decorations," Joy explained. She experienced a huge demand from mothers. "Our entire perspective on learning has changed," she said. "We've shattered what the norms for learning were in everybody's minds. As a global whole, we have realized that learning can be done differently."

Inspiring New Perspectives

Susan MacDonald's company, Inspiring New Perspectives, supports leaders of early childhood education programs. In the months prior to the pandemic, Susan's calendar had been packed with coaching and consulting. She also had many planned speaking engagements promoting her recently released book, *Inspiring Professional Growth: Empowering Strategies to Lead, Motivate, and Engage Early Childhood Teachers*. All of that instantaneously evaporated.

Susan was frightened for her business and for her family. Her adult children, all essential workers, were in positions exposing them to illness. Hearing an outpouring of confusion and despair from early childhood educational leaders, Susan also feared for them. If ever there was a time early childhood educators needed to be inspired by new perspectives, it was during those early months of the pandemic. Susan stood prepared to step in and help.

Back in 2018, Susan had begun to develop online courses as a supplement to her live work. The efforts had served her well, and she stood ready to move all of her programming online. Swiftly she created an online summit and organized weekly dialogues with leaders in the field whose programs were temporarily closed or running remotely.

Susan began by inviting leaders to pose questions to themselves:

> How can I bring who I am, what I know, and what I believe to this moment in history?
>
> How do I move through this time with grace and stay true to my work?
>
> Who do I want to be during this time? Who do I want to be when this is over?
>
> How can I use this great pause in history to refocus?

Susan then guided participants to choose a professional growth project central to their reopening plans. The range of projects included workshops for staff on teaching with positivity and joy, creating an outdoor classroom, more effectively communicating and engaging with families, and implementing COVID health and safety protocols in ways that support social-emotional health and wellness.

Long grounded in Reggio-inspired learning, even leading educational leadership retreats to Reggio Emilia, Italy, Susan asked questions very similar to those that were energizing and motivating me:

> Were we experiencing a moment analogous to the founding of the first Reggio school?
>
> Might we, like the villagers of Villa Cella, be seeing something so beautiful growing out of something so devastating?

Susan saw in the dialogues with educators and in their projects a deep sense of rejuvenation. Through connection, reflection, and planning, educators were able to transform fear and despair into hope and joy.

"Digging deep, I was able to rebuild the work that I love into the work that was needed," Susan said. The pivotal conversations she facilitated helped early childhood educators experience a sense of joyful connection in the moment, while setting a foundation for rejuvenation moving forward.

5 From Pods to Microschools

As the weeks of pandemic turned to months, we began hearing more and more talk of "pods." Initially, pods were a creative response to mitigate the risks of exposure to COVID-19, to solve challenges families had finding child care, and to let children socialize during a time of isolation. Small, consistent groups of children met without masks or physical distancing. In some pods, children participated in their own schools' distance learning programming. In other pods, privately hired teachers supplemented or even replaced learning that children would have received in school. In time, many families bid farewell to their pods and sent their children back to school. Other families decided they never wanted to go back to their previous schools. They had found quality and vision in their pods that they had not experienced before. I wondered: Were pods-turned-schools or, rather, microschools central to the founding moment for education that I sensed we were experiencing?

Microschools themselves are not new. Prior to opening Discovery Village, I had been the founding lower school director of a microschool in New York City. When I saw the position advertised in 2016, I was intrigued.

Yet at the time I had absolutely no idea what a microschool was. To prepare for the interview I had to search online for "microschool." Now I have my own definition: a microschool is a very small school with a very large vision for what learning can be.

Microschools can serve from fewer than a handful of students to about 150. Larger schools or districts can create within them a microschool, a microprogram, or even multiple microschools or microprograms, offering flexibility and choice for students and families. Whether public or private, standing on their own or even as part of larger schools, microschools have the potential to emerge as central in the post-COVID educational landscape. In the following pages, we meet four pods that continued operating even when schools reopened in person, evolving into microschools: Windsor Hill Primary School in Falmouth, Maine; Acton Academy Silicon Valley in Belmont, California; Emergent Expressions in Peru; and Sunbeam Nature School in Petaluma, California.

A New Possible

When Mary Roux Train left the public school at which she was teaching on Friday, March 13, 2020, she knew in her heart she wouldn't be back for some time. Nobody was saying it. In fact, there was an announcement that everybody would be back on Monday. Yet the virus was getting worse throughout the country and in her state of Maine.

As Mary prepared to leave for what she did not yet know would be forever, she wasn't thinking about starting her own microschool. Her thoughts were on her kindergarten students. How could she teach them if she was not physically with them? Quickly preparing, Mary printed a 200-page packet of standards-based activities. She then filled each child's backpack with the packet and about thirty books each. When the children asked why they needed to bring so much home, Mary told them that you just never know when you might not be able to make it to school.

Mary had known.

Students did not return for the rest of the academic year. Teachers came back for just two more days, the following Monday and Tuesday, to prepare to teach remotely. A shift that in the past would have taken years of planning and training happened in just two days. Mary dedicated herself to providing the best possible remote learning experience, creating a virtual classroom community with a learning app that allowed children to easily upload and share their work.

In those early days of the pandemic, Mary wasn't thinking about leaving her job. Conversation about pods had not yet reached the national vernacular. Then a family with a child entering first grade approached her with a question: "Would it be crazy to hire a private teacher?" Mary's immediate response was positive. She told the family she felt it made sense to do whatever they needed to make it through the next academic year. However, Mary added a cautionary note: be very careful choosing a teacher to ensure quality. Before long another family approached her: "What if we brought a small group of children together to learn?" Suddenly, an approach Mary had never previously imagined became a viable possibility.

After carefully considering her options, Mary started a pod for the 2020–2021 school year. Her school's rapid shift to remote learning, while successful, had been stressful. She anticipated that schools would be facing a year with ongoing shifts between remote, hybrid, and in-school learning. Her decision to leave her public school job and start a pod was rooted in her commitment to managing stress for herself and the children in her care.

Mary's pod more than flourished. "It was the most amazing year of teaching of my life," she said with joy. Teaching in her small multiage pod—just six children from three families—gave her professional autonomy and the ability to personalize learning for her students. Now she does not have to interrupt ongoing learning to take children to specialist classes at scheduled times. Assessments, while important, can happen when it works for the children. Perhaps most significantly, Mary can use an eclectic approach, carefully tailored to meet the individual needs of each of her students. Sometimes she brings out what she refers to as the boot camp style of learning, prevalent in the public schools where she has worked. Other times, she draws from what she calls the yoga style of learning, typical in the private schools where she has taught. Mary appreciates both her boot camp and her yoga approaches. She sees each as leading to health and wellness.

The pod was so successful that Mary decided she was never going back to her job. Instead she founded her own microschool with a colleague. The school's name, Windsor Hill, combines the childhood home addresses of Mary and her cofounder, who grew up on streets called Windsor Place and Snow Hill, respectively.

Windsor Hill Primary School intentionally blends school and home, learning and life. Mary is adamant about keeping Windsor Hill small. Serving only children in kindergarten and first grade, the school has no more than eight students to every one teacher and no more than twenty-four students total. Mary views Windsor Hill as a gentle step between the small, nurturing environment of preschool and the large local public school. Her vision for Windsor Hill is to "support a generation that will need to solve major problems in the world." To this end, Mary offers foundational academic skills in a small setting, personalized attention, and an emphasis on science, technology, engineering, and math (STEM), social studies, and the arts. Mary rounds out her vision with an emphasis on community service and a focus on mindset, specifically ways of being positive and engaged.

"For a long time I felt school was changing but not in the ways I think will serve children," Mary said. On her own, Mary can stand out because of what she stands for. While she respects the core academic foundation schools offer, she worries that most schools have shed other vital goals—social-emotional learning, connections with the world, and mindsets for learning. Mary has also grown distressed by how assessments are used in the public system, including their uses in informing others how a student is doing and identifying students at risk. For Mary, assessments remain important, but they are less frequent and more personalized, aimed at gaining information to tailor instruction to the needs of students.

Mary remains passionate about equity in education and hopeful that public schools will experience renewal. However, she does not see herself as the person who can spark that renewal within the large, complicated public system. "I love what I do, and I wouldn't have said that last year. I didn't realize that I had given up, lost my voice, become passive and accepting of what didn't feel right. Now I don't feel that way at all. COVID was a catalyst," Mary said. "I would not have set out and tried something new if COVID hadn't happened."

Making Learning Magical

Maria Ferrari and her husband, Brian, did not start out as educational innovators. But as it was for Mary Roux Train, COVID was the catalyst for the couple and their four daughters. Their oldest daughter's experience in Catholic school throughout kindergarten and first grade was mostly positive.

The family was by no means looking for an alternative, though Maria and Brian often contemplated the ways education could be better. Then COVID hit. Like children throughout the world, Maria's two school-age daughters found themselves quite suddenly engaged in remote learning. The change was hard. Maria and Brian had never promoted screen time, and the experience of learning fully online in kindergarten and first grade was terribly dissatisfying. Initially, Maria's mother stepped in to teach the three oldest girls, who ranged in age from four to seven. While Maria had not yet disenrolled her daughters from their school, the video conference sessions the school offered faded in importance, soon becoming a mere supplement to learning with their grandmother.

The new homeschoolers thrived. Learning became a joy again, and previous homework battles that had been part of the fabric of life at home disappeared entirely. Maria and Brian were again enjoying time with their daughters, no longer having to spend the fraction of the day they had together fighting about homework.

It was then that Brian heard a podcast about Acton Academy, a network of schools that is reimagining education by creating a deep learning, student-centered environment. The Acton organization allows individuals anywhere to apply and establish their own Acton Academy. After a rigorous application process, Maria and Brian were accepted to start their own school in Silicon Valley, and they found a partner with whom to open the school who herself has three children. The founders thus knew that with just their own children minimally they would have a founding cohort of seven. From there, they would recruit more.

In the summer of 2020, although not yet ready to launch their Acton Academy, Maria was not willing to enroll her children in a remote learning experience. She became involved with a social media group connecting families who wanted to form pods and set about putting together a pod for the 2020–2021 academic year.

Brian, a talented builder, designed learning spaces in their home. This included both a classroom and a makerspace studio in which children could tinker, design, build, and create. They interviewed a handful of individuals to be the pod's teacher, whom they referred to as a guide. After considering a range of candidates, they made an untraditional choice. Mr. Mo had never set foot as a teacher in a traditional classroom, though he had tutored for as long as he could remember. His energy and passion for learning resonated with

Maria and Brian. To enrich the children's experience further, they hired a part-time art teacher.

Maria signed on a total of ten children for her pod. Two of them were her own daughters. Her Acton cofounder's children were not part of the pod. Most of the students came from traditional schools, though a few came from Waldorf or project-based schools. All the families disenrolled from their previous schools and committed full-time to the pod for the 2020–2021 school year. Still, except for Maria's family, who would go to Acton once launched, the rest intended to return to their schools after 2020–2021. Consequently, Brian and Maria worked with Mr. Mo to create an environment and curriculum that would uphold some of the traditional school experience but still push boundaries. This included no homework, project-based learning, and mastery learning, which is an approach in which children progress at their own pace.

Within months, Maria and Brian felt the impact. *Magical* is the word Maria used to describe learning in the pod. Children found joy in reading. They thrived in math using decks of cards, a classroom economy system, and other more hands-on approaches. Students met a beekeeper, leading them to explore the effects of pollinators on the environment. A gardener came to work with them, and they explored the difference between growing plants in a greenhouse and an outdoor garden. Children gained as much insight into democracy and collaboration through proactive problem solving during recess as during what would be defined as academic time.

On Saturdays Maria's daughters couldn't wait to get back to school on Monday. They had lost this joy for learning in traditional kindergarten and first grade. "We always felt the traditional model fell short but never knew there was something else," Maria said. "We never would have imagined taking our daughters out of school without COVID. Without COVID we were stuck."

Through this time Maria worked toward opening the Acton Academy. While Acton students learn core school subjects, there is flexibility by design. There is, in Maria's words, "a clear canvas in which imagination is embraced, mistakes are embraced, and within which no child will be compared to another or made to feel inadequate." Children gain tools to problem solve and work out challenges, both in projects and in relationships. Time is dedicated to conflict resolution, and children are immersed in an environment that builds empathy.

While recruiting students to Acton, Maria understands the reservations of parents who themselves were well served following a traditional path. She recognizes that letting go of known models can be frightening. Still, even with her fears, Maria sees the changing requirements of the workforce and passionately believes in Acton's approach. "In the workforce you don't have a teacher telling you what to do," Maria said. "The information is there and what is required is not compliance but soft skills, the ability to think critically, be empathetic, work with people, solve problems, and find what we can do to help the world be a better place."

Education Aligned with Our Values

Long before the pandemic, Kaitlin Coppola recognized that her educational vision did not align with the large public school district where she served as an early childhood special education teacher and instructional coach. Increasing academic demands placed on preschoolers, who simply were not ready, left children feeling stressed and dejected. The caseloads for special education teachers were overwhelming, and teachers simply did not have the time to fully support their students. Kaitlin witnessed too many families lose faith in schools' ability to serve their children, opting instead to homeschool.

After trying to serve in a system not aligned with her vision, Kaitlin realized she could not continue to do so with integrity. She resigned from her position prior to the start of the 2019–2020 school year and set off to travel, finding her way to Peru. There she began teaching, first in a school and then as a private teacher.

With time to explore her own ideals and various educational models, Kaitlin gained clarity. In January 2020 she began Emergent Expressions Family-Centered Early Education Services. At the time she had no idea that by March the whole world would shift to what amounted to homeschooling. Through Emergent Expressions, Kaitlin coaches families and family cooperatives in creating learning experiences that align with their philosophical values. This includes families who use traditional curriculum, Montessori, inquiry-based learning, Waldorf, Reggio-inspired, forest school, and unschooling methodologies. Her ambitious mission is to assist families in re-creating educational structures in ways that are inclusive of children with a wide range of needs, including neurodiverse children.

Kaitlin also cofounded a bilingual learning community, Nueva Generación, offering self-directed learning, outdoor play opportunities, and workshops for children ages three to fourteen. The program was well received, and Kaitlin quickly began plans for an expansion. "We don't know what the future will be, but we can bet on uncertainty, change, and instability," she reflected. To prepare for that future, she passionately believes in learning that is play and project-based, incorporating social collaboration, emotional awareness, and the ability to be adaptable and resilient.

What School Has the Potential to Be

When COVID struck, Shawna Thompson's reaction was swift and confident. Like so many early childhood programs throughout the country and the globe, her younger daughter's school closed. Believing deeply that kids need to be with other kids, Shawna recognized that she could make that happen for her own two daughters and for several other children as well in her community in Petaluma, California.

Shawna had all the ingredients she needed to open her own small school: graduate training in education, experience both as an educator and a mom in Montessori, Waldorf, Reggio-inspired, and nature-based preschool programs, and a large yard. Serving a mixed-age group of six children between the ages of two and six, including her own two daughters, Shawna began operating her own nature-based preschool. Knowing that because of COVID it was safer to be outdoors, Shawna organized her preschool so that children would be out in nature all the time.

Shawna's educational approach is an eclectic blend of what she has absorbed over her years as an early childhood educator, including time she spent working in a nature-based preschool operating out of San Francisco's Presidio park as well as her participation in an early childhood educator learning experience in Reggio Emilia, Italy. Shawna appreciates the importance of slowing down and engaging in nature. She deeply values Reggio's grounding in discourse and democracy and its emphasis on teachers as researchers of children's learning.

Play, both sensory and physical, is at the core of Shawna's approach to learning. She noted research showing that physical development is the number one indicator for kindergarten readiness. From the time her daughters were infants, Shawna embraced research on the importance of allowing babies to move freely and letting them investigate and figure out their world without rescuing them too quickly.

The culture in Shawna's program is rooted in respect for and trust in children. Shawna emphasizes both communication and independent skills, and her students set goals to challenge themselves. The environment, in Shawna's words, is a "dance with children," navigating between allowing them to make choices and setting needed limits to make sure they are safe. In addition to learning about and caring for the planet, it is vital to Shawna that children learn about and care for themselves. "Nature includes being aware of yourself and your needs," Shawna said. She focused on simplifying, pushing back against what she calls the "striving" culture of our times and the many pressures that make kids consumers of their education, rather than self-directed learners.

Spending her days outside with young children, Shawna has connected to nature while reaching a painful acceptance of what it means to live on land taken from Native peoples. In age-appropriate ways, Shawna has spoken with her young students about the legacy of the First Peoples and about the color of our skin, infusing antibias learning experiences within her school.

Shawna's program was so impactful that she decided to launch her own nature-based microschool. After exploring a range of possible settings, including a historic schoolhouse and a plot of land for a fully outdoor program, Shawna decided to continue, at least for the immediate future, in the space outside her home, which backs up to a creek and forest trail. Sunbeam Nature School was officially born.

As Shawna shifts from pod to permanent microschool, she continues to think broadly and deeply about her mission, drawing on work she has done throughout her career with a range of vision-driven start-up microschools. Shawna hopes her experience inspires other parents. She herself stands in awe of how so many schools and families have responded to the constraints and challenges of COVID with innovations that meet children's needs. She views the challenging time of pandemic as potentially the beginning of something new, an opening for families to be able to think more expansively about what works for their children, forge partnerships, and advocate for what school has the potential to be.

6

Schools: Transformed Overnight

Long criticized for being incredibly slow to change, when the pandemic struck, schools transformed to remote learning quite literally overnight. Responsibility for the well-being of their students, now physically distanced, weighed heavily on administrators and teachers. They responded with compassion and resilience. Navigating through this monumental effort, staff and students alike found strengths within themselves they had not recognized before. They did not merely operate during the pandemic. They got better. In the following pages, we meet educators from a range of schools who substantially expanded their vision and the quality of learning they offer. These schools include Farmingdale School District in Farmingdale, New York; Larchmont Charter School in Los Angeles, California; Randolph School in Wappingers Falls, New York; Hudson Lab School in Hastings-on-Hudson, New York; and the Open School in Santa Ana, California.

What Regrowth Should We Protect?

As the pandemic first reached New York's shores, Dr. William Brennan, assistant superintendent for innovation and organizational development at the Farmingdale School District, found himself and his district in reactive mode. Located on the south shore of Long Island, the Farmingdale School District has an enrollment of more than 5,600 students and serves a diverse population. As leaders in such a large K–12 public school district, Bill, his superintendent, and their professional teams had always faced many demands. Yet those early days of pandemic brought a struggle unlike any other as the district shifted its students and teachers to remote learning. Initially, just getting kids to show up to their online classes was a significant challenge. In seeking a path forward, Bill reached out to a network of people who could support and inspire him.

A powerful metaphor emerged in the conversation Bill was holding with his peers and mentors. Our world had become a victim of what felt like a giant wildfire, incredibly destructive, eliminating dominant structures. With that metaphor in mind, Bill and his colleagues posed a central question. When the giant wildfire of these multiple crises passes, much will have been destroyed. Yet there will also be regrowth. As we stand in that forest after enduring devastation, *what regrowth will we be looking to protect?*

It's a seismic question. Bill described the process of protecting regrowth through a metaphor of leading from three distinct boxes.

*From **box one** leaders maintain current reality.* Bill posited that most of us spend the vast majority of our time, perhaps 95 percent, in box one. *From **box three**, leaders design the future.* This is the place of inspiration and possibility. Yet the hardest part of the work does not occur either in box one or box three. It comes from the often ignored box two: *from **box two** we let go of the past.* At some point, to embrace the new, we must abandon the past. Doing so is rarely easy.

This was Bill's experience as spring 2020 turned to summer and he worked with faculty in his district to plan for the new year. As his large district designed an opening plan that allowed students the option either to attend school in person or to continue remote learning, they faced many compliance demands, both for health and for learning. In planning, teachers worried. How would they meet required standards? What would assessment look like? Bill wanted teachers to know that, at least in the beginning weeks of school, none of that mattered. During those challenging opening days and weeks of the school year, the essential focus was building connections with the kids.

As weeks turned to months, students and teachers settled into their new reality. Bill continued to give voice to leadership from box two. He wanted teachers to let go of some of the former expectations of what school is supposed to offer and help students deal with complexities of our times: pandemic, political unrest, climate change, and the polarization of perspectives in our society.

Leading through the pandemic was "a massive test of my ability," Bill said. He and the rest of his district's leadership needed to be strategic as they were immersed in a rapid decision-making process. "It taught us to be lean—not necessarily financially but in utilization of resources and time," he explained. The demands required "new thinking, courage, trust, and vulnerability." Throughout it all, Bill and his district found themselves managing many perspectives. "Leading through times of major polarities has been a leadership challenge. It has required radical openness."

Bill reflected, with great humility and honesty, on the struggles for public school educators. Even in districts like his, with an assistant superintendent whose very job title includes innovation, there is so much compliance demanded. There is a very real gap between what educators are told they *must* do, what they feel they *should* do, and what they might achieve if given a blank slate. Still, Bill is proud of the work of his teachers, offering students the best experience possible given their circumstances and constraints.

Remote Project-Based Learning

Since she began teaching, Sara Lev has embraced the motto "Young children *can*." She is highly skilled at designing experiences that bring out the capacity both in young children and in her colleagues. Sara teaches at Larchmont Charter School in Los Angeles, California, a public school with a socioeconomically, culturally, and racially diverse community of students. Larchmont serves students from transitional kindergarten through twelfth grade. Sara teaches transitional kindergarten. Otherwise known as TK, transitional kindergarten is the first of a two-year kindergarten program offered by California public schools for children who turn five between September 1 and December 2. This unique position in TK places Sara at the intersection of early childhood and the early grades.

Sara is passionate about project-based learning, an approach in which learning occurs through active exploration of real-world challenges and problems. She is the coauthor of *Implementing Project Based Learning in Early Childhood: Overcoming Misconceptions and Reaching Success.* Sara coaches colleagues in this innovative learning approach and is a leader of a robust network of educators in early childhood and the early grades. Her professional community is primarily focused on sharing projects and resources. Much of this sharing occurs via the website she hosts with partners Amanda Clark and Erin Starkey and a large, active Facebook group: Early Childhood Project Based Learning.

At Larchmont Charter School, Sara has combined her love of experiential, learner-centered instruction with her commitment to equity through high-quality, publicly funded education. She is determined to demonstrate that equity and quality education must be available for all. "There are often assumptions about children perceived as coming from impoverished backgrounds. Project-based learning leverages their strengths and builds on them, not limiting their cognitive development," she said.

Rather than assuming her project-based approach would be impossible in a remote setting, Sara committed to figuring it out. When her class first moved to remote learning, she designed a short project-based learning unit called "Home Base," in which children designed a set of activities they could do while their parents were working. Sara's students created an online resource of activities for kids and families. As fall 2020 approached, it became clear that Sara's school would continue to operate remotely. The school leadership at Larchmont gave Sara lots of autonomy in teaching her class remotely, trusting her to make developmentally appropriate decisions for her students. Sara deeply appreciated the trust placed in her and embraced the challenge.

"I didn't think my view of what children could do could expand, but it actually did," Sara said. Daily virtual visits into each other's homes blurred the distinction between school and home, learning and life. Children loved seeing each other's rooms, meeting each other's pets and siblings, and playing together, each using their own toys.

During these visits, Sara and the children noticed a shared interest in outer space. Many had planet posters on their walls, space-themed bedsheets, or NASA T-shirts. They decided to create and produce their very own podcast about outer space. One of the many highlights of the study was a visit from a lead engineer at SpaceX. While incorporating learning standards, Sara also found a heartening increase in student agency. Children more readily advocated for themselves, asking to go to breakout rooms to learn or to participate in choice time with different materials.

Highly effective small-group work was another entirely unexpected benefit of remote learning. In imagining how to best meet children's needs, Sara dedicated mornings to full-class synchronous learning experiences and afternoons to small-group work time. In the classroom, Sara's small groups were often interrupted by the typical goings-on of the day, but in the remote learning model Sara was able to focus exclusively on the students in the group working with her. Her other students were not online at that time, instead doing independent projects on their own. The results were so dramatically positive that she resolved to replicate that focused, targeted instruction once she could teach again in a regular classroom.

One essential element of project-based learning is that learners reflect, receive feedback, and revise to create high-quality finished products. This process of thoughtful reflection, critique, and revision proved especially successful in the remote environment Sara designed. She attributed the success to the tools she integrated into the learning experience. Using a platform called Seesaw, students could post and share their work with one another, record themselves telling Sara about their work, and offer feedback to one another. The platform was effective for similar reasons as the small groups. In the classroom, Sara had to juggle many demands at once. However, in her online design, she found tools and techniques that allowed for more focused, targeted instruction. Sara recognized she could learn from her experiences teaching remotely and design for more focus within the in-person learning environment.

The experience of remote learning brought parents into the classroom in ways that never would have happened in the past. Sara embraced the partnership, holding parent meetings to help them understand her instructional approaches. She wondered about ways she might continue this positive engagement with parents once back in the classroom.

When Sara first met her students in person at a masked, socially distanced event in a park, several months into the school year, she began to cry. Seeing how small her students were, and knowing what had been required of them, overwhelmed her. At the same time, reflecting on their accomplishments, she was awed. "Your kids are blowing my mind," she shared with parents. "They are adapting, resilient, and learning."

Sara was delighted when her school reopened. When back in person, Sara emphasized social-emotional learning as well as antibias and diversity education. In learning at home for eight months, her students had missed opportunities for social interactions with peers. Sara worked with them to identify the feelings they experience in social situations. She also helped them develop language skills for sustaining relationships. Together, Sara and her students created a poetry book celebrating their identities as well as honoring and respecting their diversity.

Sara has long focused on creating a class culture emphasizing safety, belonging, and fun. She is proud of sustaining that strong, intentional culture through the pandemic. It wasn't easy. The world felt horrifically unsafe. Yet Sara's students experienced her embracing class culture even while learning remotely. "Maybe I show more patience, kindness, and flexibility. The kids too, perhaps because of what they had to navigate, are so incredibly kind, flexible, patient, and understanding."

Education as an Expression of Care

"Hope is an expression of care," relayed Josh Kaplan, director of the Randolph School, a progressive, experiential independent school in New York's Hudson Valley, serving slightly more than sixty students from pre-K to fifth grade. And for Josh, education, at its most fundamental core, is also an expression of care. Throughout the difficult months leading his school through pandemic, Josh anchored himself in that deeply held value of care. He emphasized that "providing quality learning and care through the pandemic was never a question of *if*. It was always a question of *how*."

More than any other leader with whom I spoke, Josh grounded himself in science. Throughout the pandemic, he was in frequent communication with officials at the New York State Department of Health. He also received guidance from a parent at his school who is an epidemiologist who works for the United Nations. His approach was to create the least restrictive environment possible given available scientific research about the virus.

Initially, as schools in New York and throughout the country were shifting to remote learning, Josh and his school board canceled their community-wide Maple Sugar Festival, scheduled for Saturday, March 14, 2020, and closed school for what they anticipated would be a week or maybe two. As the weeks drew on and New York was featured in the news as a global COVID hotspot, it became apparent to Josh that his school's closure was going to last significantly longer than several weeks. He worked long hours to determine how to serve students when they could not physically come to school. His wife's job as a therapist had also grown dramatically busier as pandemic stress took a substantial toll on many of her patients. The couple worked primarily from home while parenting their two children, a preschooler who would have been attending Randolph and an infant. The days were long and focused on giving care: Josh to his community, his wife to her patients, and both to their children. Self-care seemed a distant dream. In that hectic reality, Josh and his wife were by no means alone.

Josh's social media feed was blowing up with posts from panicked parents, seemingly seeking to outdo each other in who would be the best homeschooling family. The intensity of it all affected Josh profoundly. Reflecting on what was transpiring around him, he came to a reassuring realization. Living and learning are interdependent conditions. Josh wanted to tell parents not to turn to the internet for lesson plans but to learn with their children through daily experiences. The possibilities for living Randolph's approach of hands-on, experiential, interdisciplinary learning while at home resonated deeply for Josh, both as an educator and as a parent. Yet he recognized that very few parents felt comfortable weaving life and learning together. To assist, he launched a weekly community video conference meeting for families, sharing a message of nonjudgmental care and offering ideas for low-stress learning opportunities at home.

Grounding his pandemic response in Randolph's understanding of education as care, his initial focus was on bringing familiarity to children during profoundly unfamiliar times. Alongside his faculty and leadership team, Josh designed a full menu of live and on-demand learning opportunities. This included video conferences in the morning, lunchtime video meetups for children to socialize, and a range of interest-based elective learning opportunities including dance, gardening, art, and music sessions. The most popular session was a read-aloud led by a beloved retired Randolph teacher. Through it all, the Randolph community formed new traditions and celebrations together.

Although he was providing meaningful opportunities for self-directed learning, Josh understood that Randolph's children needed to return to school. Making connections with colleagues and expert advisers throughout the world, he gained insight from the experiences of others to provide the safest environment possible. Josh benefited tremendously from the virtual dialogues facilitated by Boulder Journey School. Those interactions with colleagues validated Josh's own planning process with his teachers and helped him inspire his teachers to remain motivated and excited about innovating.

At times Josh felt despondent. On one of those occasions in April 2020, one of Randolph's trustees, who had taught at the school, came to visit. Sitting outside together on Randolph's empty campus, the trustee shared stories of the school's past. He described how, back in the 1970s, teachers enjoyed staff retreats camping out together in lean-tos. An image came to Josh's mind of lean-tos on campus with children learning inside them.

Energized, Josh convinced his trustees to purchase seven lean-to structures. He would assign one cohort of children to each structure and place the structures far enough apart so cohorts could maintain physical distance from one another. In addition, Josh moved forward with previous plans to build an outdoor amphitheater. The amphitheater would be large enough for the entire community to come together, with room for physical distancing between cohorts.

Josh then turned his attention to caring for his staff. He recognized that the summer jobs Randolph teachers typically found to supplement their income would not be available in the COVID environment. Thus, although Randolph teachers typically receive a salary only during the ten months of school, he paid them for the summer of 2020. While the larger world felt as though it was burning, it was vital to Josh that in his own small world people take care of each other.

Fall brought the beginning of what the community called the Randolph Revival. The effort occurred in three distinct phases: reopening, winter, and reemergence. In phase one, children returned to school and learned in their outdoor lean-tos. Despite the turbulence of the outside world, Josh was awed by how incredibly peaceful it was at Randolph, with space for comfortable distancing and a focus on joyful learning.

With the onset of winter, Randolph Revival phase two began. Learning continued primarily outdoors. Each learning cohort was assigned an indoor space for the coldest days. "We have some really strong kids," Josh shared with genuine appreciation. "They were resilient in ways we were amazed by," showing up to school in full winter gear and embracing outdoor learning all day every day. The approach delighted Randolph's families and resonated with many prospective families too, including some already living locally looking for alternative learning options and others moving out of New York City to the Hudson Valley and looking for a school.

Facing the economic turbulence that coincided with the pandemic, Josh took a bold step in designing a new model for tuition. He called it Stone Soup, modeled on the story of people bringing what they can to create a soup for all to share. Some bring carrots while others bring prime rib. The six-tiered tuition model charges based on an algorithm that determines what a family can afford. The model has reduced tuition for 75 percent of families and eliminated financial aid. It nurtures justice and equity, eliminating distinctions between full-paying and scholarship students. For Josh, the intensity of COVID brought with it an "opportunity to do things differently, looking at this time as our moment to become a Stone Soup school." It seems to be working, resonating with the community and resulting in approximately the same tuition income coming in as in the school's previous tuition- and scholarship-based model.

The Herculean efforts took their toll on Josh. "Randolph is a small organization, and I wear every hat," he said. He has no office staff and conveyed that at times the workload feels impossible, even debilitating. "Everyone teaches that we should practice self-care, but there is just not enough time. It's not possible to work more, and I am tired all the time." Still, he is proud of how much he and his school have grown. "It's a process. Learning is a process. Growth is a process. The community has grown so much. We've come quite a distance. Trust has grown. People are paying attention."

When winter turned to spring, a feeling of joy and accomplishment permeated the Randolph community. The signature Maple Sugar Festival was finally back, and it would be a grand celebration—but with a significant twist. Although Randolph had always opened the festival to the broader community, in 2021 it was exclusively for staff, students, and their families. While it had always been an opportunity to fundraise, in 2021 it would be purely celebratory, welcoming parents and vaccinated grandparents onto campus.

People often asked Josh when he thought things at Randolph would return to normal. He would smile and respond, "They won't." While the high-level health protocols would no longer be required post-pandemic, the environment of calm, the embrace of learning outdoors, the creative problem solving, and the strengthening of connection between learning and life have had a permanent positive impact. The Randolph Revival transcended COVID, propelling the school community to a place in which members even more authentically live their vision of what learning and life can be.

Students as the Drivers of Their Own Learning

In 2017, several years before much of the world turned to pods and microschools as viable learning options, wife and husband team Cate Han and Stacey Seltzer opened Hudson Lab School, the school they dreamed of for their own two daughters. The couple had grown disillusioned with school when their older daughter was in first grade. Not finding what they wanted and being entrepreneurs themselves, they became, in Stacey's words, "naive enough to think we could create our own school."

The school's unique setting, in rented rooms in the Andrus on Hudson nursing home, contributed to its inspiring culture from the very start. Teachers and the eleven pioneering students, two of whom were Cate and Stacey's daughters, developed close connections with the nursing home residents they lovingly refer to as "the grands." The nursing home's expansive outdoor space encouraged meaningful connections with nature and the environment.

From the start, Cate and Stacey embraced interdisciplinary, project-based learning as the primary mode of learning at Hudson Lab School. Within the model, children learn content and skills in the process of completing an ambitious project. Rather than taking tests or writing papers, students prepare an exhibition for the community, including parents, grandparents, and others. In designing Hudson Lab School, Cate and Stacey aimed to prepare their students to become lifelong learners who can adapt and thrive in all sorts of situations. "We had no idea the intensity of the challenges our students would face or that those challenges would show up so quickly," Stacey reflected. Pandemic stress tested Hudson Lab School's approach, he said. Both he and Cate were tremendously proud of how well their students demonstrated adaptability and resilience in the face of challenge and change.

"While our worlds literally felt as though they had turned upside down, there was a huge difference from the experiences of others and of how our community came together," Cate shared. "Our students mostly thrived because they had been prepared to be the drivers of their own learning." They embraced choice in activities and projects at home, including creating films and stories, learning origami, and reaching out to relatives who might be lonely. One student produced an elaborate talent show, bringing the school community together and celebrating the interests and abilities of her classmates. "We have a deep level of pride in how the community is coming together," Cate said. "I am so proud of our kids for their ability to find joy for themselves."

During this time of isolation, as residents in nursing homes were at high risk of depression, the relationship between Hudson Lab School and the grands flourished. While Hudson Lab School students were learning virtually and were not permitted to visit the grands in person, they remained connected. First graders discussed the link between scent and memory and made sachets with lavender or coffee beans and sent them as gifts to the grands. The older students explored the topic of aging and ageism. "The connections both deepened students' empathy and helped the grands battle loneliness and isolation," said Hudson Lab School's intergenerational program coordinator, Joanne Corrigan.

In the fall of 2020, Hudson Lab School resumed in-person learning. On the expansive grounds of the Andrus on Hudson nursing home, educators set up outdoor tents for each classroom. In planning the return, it was vital to Cate and Stacey that everyone in the community—students, families, and teachers—felt heard, seen, and cared for. Health and safety were their highest priority. Children and teachers alike adapted, becoming even more interested in science, especially climate science. They watched the effect of the pandemic on people and on the planet, recognizing both the pain as well as the unintended benefit of lower carbon emissions.

"The pandemic brought education into everyone's living rooms," Stacey said. "It opened parents' minds to considering alternatives and spending more time thinking about the best option for their child. Previously people just sent their child to the local public school. The pandemic totally shook that up."

Local Connection and Global Reach

When in March 2020 schools suddenly shut down, there was no thought that a Sudbury school could possibly function in a virtual space. The hallmark of Sudbury schools—self-directed democratic learning stemming from organic interactions within the community—did not easily translate into a remote environment. For most of the approximately seventy schools throughout the world that are modeled after Sudbury Valley School in Framingham, Massachusetts, the task seemed impossible. Whether or not schools strove to remain open with responsible COVID health and safety protocols, many Sudbury students and families disconnected from their school communities. Some Sudbury schools simply shut down. Yet Cassandra Clausen, who in 2015 founded the Open School, a Sudbury school in Southern California, was determined to find a way to continue to serve remotely while remaining true to her school's powerful democratic approach.

"We always believed we had to have a campus—and be in person—for this community-based democratic model in which kids create their own environment," Cassandra said. Yet, due to the specific health needs of many in the Open School community, resisting a virtual option would have meant losing connection with the majority of the school's families. Cassandra reached out to coaches and mentors who supported her to dive deep, shifting her mindset and opening her thinking. Cassandra asked a new question: Could the Open School experience be accessible globally while still maintaining the option of on-campus learning?

Members of the Open School community worked together to design self-directed, democratic, virtual learning experiences. They transferred as much as they could from the components of pre-COVID learning that mattered most to them into a virtual space. This included a wide range of student-hosted activities and a weekly meeting with an adviser for each student. "Some children have thrived in the environment, and others have not," Cassandra reflected. She observed that some children found it easier to make connections virtually and actually formed deeper friendships than they had enjoyed in the past. Other children missed in-person connection terribly and struggled with a sense of isolation.

At times, the Open School has attracted students with anxiety or depression as they intentionally opted out of the high-pressure competitive environments of other schools. Cassandra and her team have sought to make their school an embracing and safe place, offering a range of accommodations for students, such as flexibility in attendance for children who need time to tend to their mental health. Faculty do their best to be attuned, intentionally nurturing a safe, nonjudgmental environment in which students can share their struggles, not only academic but emotional as well.

Learning through the pandemic opened new possibilities for the Open School. In the midst of the pandemic, as they planned to bring students back to campus, they also created a virtual, international community of students by opening remote learning enrollment to students anywhere in the world. Making her powerful self-directed democratic learning model accessible to as many people as possible has long been vitally important to Cassandra. However, experiences during the pandemic opened her mind to a far more expansive vision of accessibility. Initially, Cassandra had defined accessibility primarily as financial equity, seeking to include students from a wide range of socioeconomic backgrounds. To an extent, she had considered geographic accessibility, ensuring the school was accessible by bus so that families and staff who did not have cars could be part of the community. With the successful shift to remote learning, Cassandra imagined including students from rural, suburban, and urban locations throughout the globe, learning together and sharing their worlds with one another.

The Open School staff have experimented with existing and emerging technological tools and platforms to nurture interactions virtually that had previously been imaginable only in person. "I feel very changed," Cassandra reflected. "I am now more willing to be out there with my opinions and put a stake in the ground with my school about what we believe and don't believe. I feel less pressure to meet everyone's needs and desires."

7 Beyond School

Public and private K–12 schools are not the only places children learn. For many families, religious education supplements the learning children receive in school. During COVID, some faith-based organizations stepped in to do much more. Additionally, some families forged entirely new paths, creating opportunities for learning in models that were not school at all but rather co-learning communities, places in which individuals of all ages learn together. Co-learning communities at times supplement and at times entirely replace school. Offering new possibilities and choices, co-learning communities make it possible for adults and children to take ownership of their own learning in a community that nurtures strong and meaningful relationships.

This chapter introduces two innovative programs that flourished during the pandemic: Temple Beth Shalom in Needham, Massachusetts, and My Reflection Matters Village, a virtual co-learning community offering a wide range of opportunities for learning and connection, primarily for BIPOC homeschooling families.

Possibility in Community

Like many houses of worship, Temple Beth Shalom is far more than a place where people gather to pray. The large suburban synagogue, located in Needham, Massachusetts, offers a robust array of spiritual, academic, and social activities, including many opportunities for youth from preschool through high school. Temple Beth Shalom deliberately does not call its program a "religious school." The majority of the community's approximately six hundred K–12 children attend local public schools. Youth are invited to attend learning and social programming at the synagogue, typically after school and on weekends.

When the pandemic struck, Temple Beth Shalom's first response was to move youth programming online. Like schools throughout the country, they hastily put together what Rachel Happel, director of K–12 learning, described as a "decent" online learning program. Yet Rachel and her colleagues were convinced they could do better. Sarah Damelin, both a program director at the synagogue and the mother of three children who attend youth programming, conveyed the bold commitment her colleagues made to families: at the end of the pandemic, the synagogue's educational leadership wanted them to look back and share that it was Temple Beth Shalom that got them through.

Educators at Temple Beth Shalom set out to uncover what families and children in the community needed most. It quickly became evident that one size would not fit all. Based on their conversations with families, they redesigned their programs substantially.

A sizable number of families and youth longed for in-person programming. Local public schools were mostly offering hybrid options, some days in school and other days remote. This left many working families without quality child care on days children were not in school. Other families who did not need child care still longed for safe ways for their children to participate in a social community. Temple Beth Shalom offered solutions for both child care and safe social engagement.

Serving children safely became the synagogue's top priority. While Temple Beth Shalom already had an early childhood center and an after-school care program for elementary school children, the synagogue hired more staff to meet demand. At the request of families of graduating preschoolers who did not want a hybrid kindergarten experience, Temple Beth Shalom offered full-day kindergarten. It extended the after-school care program, welcoming elementary school children for care after school and during the school day when they were assigned to remote learning by their public school. Children attended their public school online sessions and completed independent work assigned by their school while also engaging in Jewish learning and lots of play, much of it outdoors.

Some families did not need child care but longed for the social engagement and learning in the community their children had enjoyed prior to the pandemic. Convinced by the growing research on the transmission of the virus that outdoor learning would be safer, the synagogue rented space at a local day camp for its Sunday learning program for elementary and middle school students. As the cold New England winters presented a formidable challenge, they planned for immersive learning on Sundays, offering five-hour days on six Sundays in the fall and six more Sundays in the spring. This was instead of a two-hour program that ran weekly from September to June. Anticipating that maybe forty children would register, staff were surprised when approximately two hundred signed up. Sixth and seventh graders also wanted to participate in the program, which had originally been designed for first through fifth graders. The synagogue obliged, renting space at a second day camp to accommodate middle school youth. Teachers and students alike responded enthusiastically and said they wanted the program to become a permanent offering, not only a response to the pandemic. It thus continued into the 2021–2022 school year as a popular option for families. Eighth graders and high school students wanted to continue attending programs on weeknights as they had pre-pandemic, so the synagogue offered outdoor learning and social programming in the parking lot two evenings a week. Youth brought their own dinner and beach chairs to learn and socialize with one another outdoors during the fall and spring months.

Temple Beth Shalom continued offering online learning for children from first through seventh grades. While this option was most similar to remote learning happening at many schools, the organization worked to make the approach as engaging and interactive as possible. Some families did not want to send their children to in-person learning during the pandemic yet were fatigued by online learning. They wanted an option for at-home learning that did not involve a screen. Educators at Temple Beth Shalom created a monthly box with curricular materials, instructions, and resources. A coach checked in monthly with families to offer support, assess progress, and keep learners accountable. Participating families loved the experience, as it brought learning home, enabling families to join together in substantive, hands-on activities.

Temple Beth Shalom had long been willing to rethink its approach, and this openness served them well through the pandemic. About a decade earlier, the synagogue's educational leadership team had recognized a substantial disparity in priorities between educators and families: the synagogue had designed a youth learning program based on Jewish educational content knowledge, but families shared that they were primarily seeking community, engagement, and relationship. With this realization, Temple Beth Shalom redesigned its programming. Over the years it continuously reflected on ways to be ever more responsive to the needs of the community. When crisis struck, they stood prepared and not only navigated through but got better.

A Place of Acceptance for BIPOC Families

My Reflection Matters Village is a virtual co-learning community, a place in which people of all ages learn together, primarily serving BIPOC homeschooling families. Founded by social justice educator and equity consultant Chemay Morales-James, the village is a place of acceptance for BIPOC families and educators. An inclusive space, the village welcomes white members who embrace the role of coconspirator, taking intentional action in living the mission of the village. Much attention is given in the village to what *co-learning*, *liberation*, and *decolonization* mean.

Prior to founding My Reflection Matters Village, Chemay served for many years as an equity coach for New York University's Metropolitan Center for Research on Equity and the Transformation of Schools. She also began her own journey as a mother, seeking to ground her children within her family's Puerto Rican and Trinidadian heritages. Through both her professional and personal journeys, Chemay found many schools well-intentioned yet ill-equipped to create environments that nurture the racial and ethnic identities of children of color and to intentionally challenge systems of oppression. Too often Chemay found that schools provided narrow representation, misrepresentation, or complete exclusion of BIPOC children and cultures from traditional curricula and media. More seriously, she found that most schools did not create a space where BIPOC children could be free to be their full selves without consequences.

Chemay made two choices, one professional and one personal. She began her own equity consulting business, providing learning materials, resources, and educational services affirming the rich lived experiences of BIPOC children and cultures, and she began home educating her own children. At first neither went as she had hoped. Professionally, Chemay felt she was not getting to the root of the racial and equity challenges in schools. She described a frustrating sense of trimming the branches of a tree whose roots had rotted when she wanted to plant new seeds. Personally, Chemay and her children experienced a similar sense of exclusion, marginalization, and misunderstanding within the predominantly white homeschooling community as they had experienced in school. She longed for freedom to have explicit conversations about oppression and spaces in which her children's heritages and cultures would be celebrated. Chemay imagined a village in which the BIPOC community, especially the BIPOC homeschooling community, could offer care to one another.

Chemay started a group on Facebook for BIPOC families which quickly grew. The group assisted BIPOC homeschooling families in finding one another and decreasing their feelings of isolation. Two members of that Facebook group, Tamsyn Ambler and Cecilia Cruz Brooks, shared their own journeys in compelling ways.

Tamsyn was, from the start, dedicated to providing her biracial children with a high-quality education and meaningful social and cultural connection with other children of color. The path to achieve this was by no means obvious. In diverse, urban Bridgeport, Connecticut, the local public schools would offer the connection with children and families of color so important to Tamsyn. Alternatively, homeschooling would enable her to give her children the quality, self-directed education she wanted for them. Yet homeschooling had a significant drawback. Most of the local homeschool community members were white families, coming from backgrounds of wealth and privilege and holding conservative values unlike hers. She recognized it would be difficult to find the connection she longed for, both for her children and for herself, among other homeschooling families. Still, weighing the pros and cons, Tamsyn elected to homeschool.

While Tamsyn found connection with BIPOC homeschooling families through Chemay's Facebook group, she longed for more. As a white woman

married to a Black man, with their family of three biracial children, Tamsyn sought connection with others whose experiences were similar to hers. Yet she felt strongly that she could not be the one to start the community she envisioned. Tamsyn explained that she is committed to being an ally and coconspirator in an education of liberation for BIPOC children. However, as a white woman, she cannot shed her privilege or assume that families of color would necessarily trust her. Over time, Tamsyn's sense of urgency for a more diverse community for her children grew. She longed for a community that was committed to affirming all identities, particularly LGBTQ children and families.

Like Tamsyn, Cecilia deliberated whether to homeschool. Dedicated to providing her children with an emotionally safe and decolonized education, Cecilia worried whether she could offer that at home. When her older son was ready for kindergarten, she initially enrolled him in public school. It did not take long for her to grow alarmed by her son's experience. Her independent child who had always loved learning grew increasingly frustrated and resistant to school. He had taught himself to read at age four and wanted to select his own books. Yet his teacher wanted him to read only the books the school was using. Cecilia's son wanted to make choices about both what and how he learned, and the school environment did not embrace self-directed learning. She made the decision to homeschool.

Initially, Cecilia worried. She felt insecure about whether she was capable of teaching her child, primarily because she felt she still had decolonizing work to do herself. As she immersed herself in homeschooling, she felt constant amazement observing her children teaching themselves new things. Her younger son, whom she homeschooled from the start, taught himself to read. As both children followed their own curiosity, their love of learning naturally blossomed. "As parents, we just have to learn and deschool ourselves from colonized and *schoolish* ideas, so that we can trust our children and trust in their ability to self-direct," Cecilia shared. *Schoolish* is a word invented in the village that means acting too much like a traditional school does. "While I was already on a decolonizing and deschooling journey, had it not been for My Reflection Matters Village, I would not be fully immersed in self-directed education," Cecilia said.

Over time online interaction among members of Chemay's Facebook group led organically to meetups and culturally relevant programming. Families began requesting an in-person co-op in which families and children could connect with each other and design learning experiences. Chemay moved forward, and the co-op for BIPOC families quickly reached maximum capacity for its rented space. With thirty-five children from about fifteen families, Chemay opened a wait list.

Soon COVID pushed much of the world to remote learning. Chemay's co-op had some outdoor meetups and engaged even more robustly online. In the quest to continue the community, she connected with 100 Roads, a program that shows families ways to create co-learning communities. Options for learning and engagement in the virtual village blossomed, and My Reflection Matters Village was born.

Chemay migrated her Facebook group to Mighty Networks, a platform offering much more flexibility and possibility for her growing global village. Members have access to culturally responsive learning resources, and children participate in online and hands-on learning experiences, stemming from their interests and connected to their cultures. For example, Chemay's and Cecilia's children became involved in the village cooking club, learning food traditions from BIPOC cultures.

Chemay structured My Reflection Matters Village as a social impact business, seeking to build wealth for the community. She invests in the community, paying partners to offer classes. She sets fees on a sliding scale, and some individuals sponsor other families, helping provide equitable access to the many services the village offers.

In time, My Reflection Matters Village has attracted a diverse national and even international audience, far beyond the membership of the initial Facebook group. Dominique DjeDje is one of the newer members of My Reflection Matters Village. She learned about the village while listening to *Fare of the Free Child*, a weekly podcast produced by author and thought leader Akilah Richards. At the time, Dominique was seeking a school or alternative learning setting. Her eighth-grade daughter had been enrolled in a public program in California that combined remote and in-person learning long before COVID brought that innovative model into the mainstream. Dominique's daughter, self-directed in areas of particular interest but not in overall academics, was not completing her assignments. A conversation with program educators about her daughter's failure to complete her work was looming.

Feeling adrift and alone, Dominique hoped My Reflection Matters Village would be exactly what she needed, and she applied for membership.

From the start, in her interview with Chemay and Tamsyn, Dominique felt connected. Feeling quickly at ease, she shared with Chemay and Tamsyn that she had so many questions and wanted answers. The pair laughed, kindly yet firmly sharing that while they did not have answers, they suspected that by engaging with other village members, Dominique would find what she sought.

Connecting in a place in which she can be unapologetically Black, no matter who else is in the room, has been powerful for Dominique. "I don't have a lot of Black spaces," she shared. This space was particularly important in the days following the murder of George Floyd. While Dominique had heard of police brutality many times, "George Floyd's death rocked me to my core, and I lay flat for two weeks," she said. Being able to participate in a workshop open only to Black women offered a connection that Dominique longed for during those painful days. Living in California, she was physically distant from many of the original group members, including Chemay. Yet the format of the village on the Mighty Networks app enabled meaningful connection.

"I've been part of homeschool co-ops in the past, and what Chemay is doing is completely different," Cecilia explained. She loves how children create and discuss what they want to learn. "Other homeschool co-ops were like mini schools," Cecilia said. In addition, she found the curriculum in other co-ops to be almost exclusively focused on the works of white authors and white artists, lacking the diversity so vital to her. Self-directed, culturally relevant learning has made a dramatic, positive difference. Cecilia has been amazed to see how the shyer children have gained confidence, sharing their learning with others.

Perhaps the most important work of the village is occurring for parents. Members have many conversations about materials in the resource library, they ask for advice, and they share experiences. Healing is essential within the village, and healers in the community offer advice, counseling, and spiritual support. Chemay explained that families in the village are dismantling what they had learned in school. "We are liberating ourselves as caregivers. There is a lot of unlearning and relearning we need to do as parents decolonizing our parenting. Many families are coming for that support."

As relationships have strengthened, parents in the village are less afraid to say what they need. Programming for parents has flourished. Among the highlights have been fireside chats, tapping into Indigenous practices of learning through storytelling. Topics for programs have included what it means to be in a community virtually while feeling isolated physically, decolonization, movement meditation, raising nonsexist boys, building wealth through the stock market, and so much more. Members together watched the video "My Grandmother's Hands," about how racialized trauma affects our bodies, and talked about it afterward in breakout racial affinity groups.

"My kids don't know much about My Reflection Matters Village. It's really for me," Dominique shared. "All of these moms are going through the same thing. In the end, just knowing somebody else is going through this helps."

For Cecilia, learning in the village has been liberating, not only for her children but for her. "COVID allowed me to let go and jump into self-led education," she explained. She has learned alongside her children and developed her own confidence and pride as a homeschooling mom. Cecilia has explored a range of educational approaches, arriving at an eclectic self-directed model that includes a wide array of Black and Latinx authors and artists.

Tamsyn reflected on how COVID forced creativity in incredibly positive ways. She has found it meaningful to connect with other white parents raising biracial children. Additionally, within the village she has found a space where parents heal from their own traumas together. Families have relied on one another throughout the pandemic and through the powerful cultural shift happening around racial justice. As Tamsyn eloquently said, "We are healing, growing, and creating together."

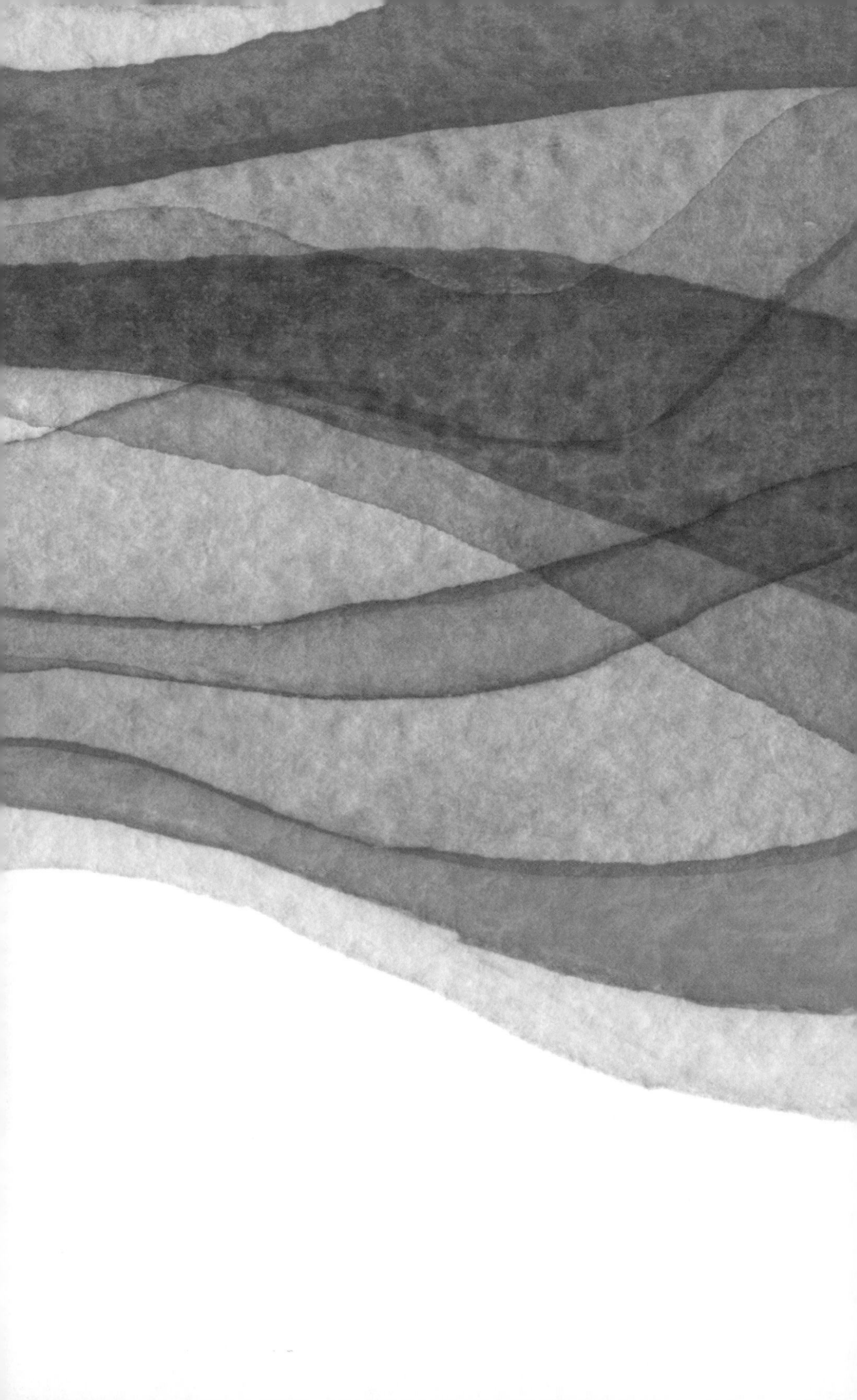

Part Three

Igniting the Best Within Ourselves and Within Our Schools

8

Sparks Leading to Transformation

Experiencing the many challenges of pandemic, protest, economic uncertainty, and extreme weather in 2020 and 2021, we learned so much. Perhaps most significant is knowing that we can face adversity and find our way through. In the process, we can improve, not only incrementally but exponentially. We can make choices for the learning and care of our students and our own children, make decisions about our careers, expand our impact both in the lives of our students and in the broader field, and design lives we love. We can stand out by what we stand for, bringing our vision and our values to life both professionally and personally.

Initially, I didn't have the language to express the approaches of educators and parents who not only navigated through the pandemic but got better. Determined to embed the wisdom we had gained into our ways of learning, serving, teaching, and leading, I wanted to describe the pathway to success we had traveled. I wanted to explore further whether we might be standing at a founding moment for education, the beginning of something new. We had endured so much and learned so much in the process. Our next chapters were yet to be written. Could we stand on the shoulders of Maria Montessori, Rudolf Steiner, and Loris Malaguzzi? Could we bring our own new approaches to learning to life, addressing the needs and possibilities of our own day? Could insights from all we had gone through offer us the foundation on which to build for the future?

Wanting to describe what we had done, so that we could learn from it in the days ahead, I created a word: REVABILITIES™.

While born during the pandemic, glimpses of REVABILITIES existed earlier. It began in my dissatisfaction with vision statements, mission statements, and lists of core values. It's not that I don't believe in them; quite the reverse: I view myself as being highly guided by vision, mission, and core values. It's just that the statements I had crafted or contributed to throughout my career had never felt adequate. They sounded too similar to other programs, falling short in their efforts to convey how the schools I was leading stood out by what they stood for.

When I created Discovery Village, I wanted more. I set out to design a framework, specific enough to guide my school yet open enough to incorporate multiple perspectives and grow with us. In addition to vision, mission, and core values, I created a fourth category. I called it *pillars*. At the time, I identified three pillars: relationships, experiences, and values. With the acronym REV, these three pillars revved up the vision I had for Discovery Village Childcare and Preschool.

Viewing the successes of the people who told their stories in this book through the lens of REV, the ways they fueled learning and care during times of adversity, I wondered whether these three pillars could serve as a framework. I imagined REV being a fabric we could weave and then tailor, dressing our programs with our own style out of the meaningful relationships, experiences, and values that ignite our own visions.

Delving further into our stories, I found I needed more. REV was good but not good enough. Expanding upon my three pillars, I created the REVABILITIES framework. The letters in REVABILITIES stand for the core tenets we relied on to navigate through the daunting challenges we faced. Each of the letters or group of letters conveys not one but two pillars. Now I had twelve guiding pillars, organized into six pairs:

R: relationships and responsiveness

E: experiences and environment

V: vision and values

A: adversity and authenticity

B: budget and busy-ness

ILITIES: abilities and possibilities

Instead of having only a mission statement and a list of core values, we think about our work in relation to these twelve pillars. Then when we make a decision or self-assess or change course, we ground ourselves in the twelve pillars as we design our path forward.

COVID sparked growth leading to transformation in ways we had not anticipated.

For some, COVID was a **catalyst**, leading us in directions we would not have otherwise ventured. Our experiences revealed possibilities for our schools and even for our lives that we had not previously imagined.

For others, COVID was an **accelerator**, propelling us forward on pathways we had already longed to embark upon.

Still others experienced COVID as an **anchor**, rooting us in our own powerful values and vision, strengthening our way of being in the world.

Finally, some experienced COVID as a **sculptor**, chipping back layers of ourselves. In removing what no longer served, we were able to uncover the essential and live more authentically, both personally and professionally.

Frequently we experienced COVID in more than one of these roles simultaneously. Most significantly, COVID showed us that we can intentionally embrace adversity to ignite growth. Having already navigated through overwhelming obstacles, becoming better in the process, we can choose to do so over and over again. COVID taught us how very capable we are.

Catalyst

COVID catalyzed massive and immediate change in education. Shutting the doors to physical buildings, schools shifted to remote learning literally overnight. The accomplishment would have taken years had we not been compelled to make it happen immediately. There were additional remarkable accomplishments. For example, for decades educators and politicians alike bemoaned the digital divide, the lack of computing devices and internet access for families living in poverty. When the pandemic hit, large urban districts found ways to distribute computing devices and obtain internet access for all students within months. The feat was a monumental accomplishment.

Some of us began to glimpse long-term possibilities for remote learning. Cassandra Clausen, founder of the Open School, who initially could not imagine her democratic learning model working outside of a physical community, is a prime example. During the pandemic Cassandra forged forward with plans to make her school accessible to any student anywhere in the world. Her example has the potential to inspire partnerships between schools internationally, engaging students in learning locally while connecting globally in shared learning experiences.

COVID likewise catalyzed radical responsiveness locally. Jenna Maggard, director of Muck and Wonder, transformed her parent-participation preschool into a full-day nature program for school-age children because that is what her local community most needed. K–12 director Rachel Happel and her colleagues at Temple Beth Shalom transformed their learning options, recognizing that for their community one size would not fit all. The models serve as examples for how community-based schools and organizations can become even more responsive to local needs.

Dissatisfied with the options available to them, educators and families began their own schools. They created learning models that brought energy and joy, ushering in lifestyles they had previously only dreamed of for themselves and for their families.

COVID showed us that choice is possible. We can design a school or an alternative learning program and a life we love even when facing overwhelming adversity. We adapted creatively and resourcefully during COVID, and we can continue to do so, not because we have to, but because we choose to.

Accelerator

Some experienced COVID as an accelerator, shaving months and even years off ambitious goals we had set for ourselves and for our schools. We experienced this acceleration in a range of ways: as a push, as a pause, as an inspiration, and as a magnet.

For many, acceleration came as a push. Already reimagining what education could be, Chemay Morales-James, founder of My Reflection Matters Village, shared that COVID "pushed us to dive deeper in that reimagining. I don't know if it would have happened or if it would have happened as quickly." At Farmingdale School District in New York, Bill Brennan, assistant superintendent, led the way for large districts to offer remote learning in creative ways even beyond COVID. This included increasing interdisciplinary inquiry-based and project-based learning opportunities. At Randolph School, director Josh Kaplan revolutionized equity and finance for independent schools with his Stone Soup six-tiered model for assessing tuition. Educators at Boulder Journey School accelerated their commitment to connecting educators with one another, promoting anti-racist and antibias teaching, and providing graduate-level online learning.

For some, acceleration came as a pause. By putting a pause on reopening and spending a full month planning with staff, pedagogical leader Jessica Holder at Discovery Child Care Centre and her team gained tremendous momentum in implementing a strategic plan that they had started forming before COVID. "We always have great ideas but never the time or human capacity" to do what was needed to reflect, plan, and implement, explained Jessica. COVID offered the gift of time to refuel in order to then accelerate.

For others, acceleration came in the form of inspiration. Susan MacDonald, founder of Inspiring New Perspectives, witnessed accelerated impact for her adult students, leaders of early childhood education programs. Working together with Susan's guidance, they inspired one another to adopt new perspectives. They gained a greater sense of self-efficacy and dramatically accelerated the intentional development of their vision and their projects.

Finally, for some, acceleration came in the form of a magnet, attracting attention to their offerings far faster than they anticipated. Kaye Boehning, director of Tomorrow's Promise; Cate Han and Stacey Seltzer, cofounders of Hudson Lab School; Joy Anderson, owner of Preschool System and Preschool

All Stars Membership; and my very own Discovery Village Childcare and Preschool saw interest in our programs increase dramatically.

COVID revealed how adversity can accelerate progress toward ambitious goals. Having experienced that acceleration, we can choose to accelerate yet again as we face the challenges still to come.

Anchor

In the face of daunting challenges and overwhelming adversity, many of us anchored ourselves in the core of what we had long seen as most essential.

Some of us were anchored in our values. Karina Wyllie, owner of Koala Park Daycare, spoke of being "solid in who we are, aligned in love, affection, nurturing, connections, and relationships." Kaye Boehning emphasized being anchored in the values of her faith and the original mission of her school. As Dominique DjeDje, a member of My Reflection Matters Village, said, "It's nice to be able to live out loud in the ways you believe and in the values you have. I feel I'm finally home."

Others were anchored in our approaches to learning. Core to Hudson Lab School is a commitment to providing children with tools to navigate difficult situations. While Cate and Stacey imagined that those difficult situations for their students would occur in the future, seeing their model support the children and community through the pandemic affirmed their approach. The experience "has given us so much conviction that what we are doing is right," Cate said.

Bill Brennan found an anchor in the innovative programming his district offers. For Bill, this includes his district's career and technical education and its advanced placement programming. The time of pandemic "strengthened what we believe is important," he said.

Still others were anchored through being fully in the moment with our students. Sara Lev, a transitional kindergarten teacher, served as an anchor as she created an environment where her students had the freedom to grow. Shawna Thompson, founding director of Sunbeam Nature School, anchored her students by "getting super present" with them, fully engaged in nature. Prior to the pandemic, Shawna had been so busy that she hadn't allowed learning to emerge in quite the same way. By slowing down she found how powerful becoming present in the moment can be.

Some were anchored in community. My Reflection Matters Village developed over the months of pandemic into a community serving the adults as much as or perhaps even more than the children. "We were healing more as adults, which helped us with parenting. We were more calm and present to see strengths in our kids with a new lens, a new look," reflected Chemay Morales-James.

Others were anchored in shared experiences. At Kaleidoscope Community School, facing COVID, fires, ice storms, windstorms, and stolen yurts "rooted us, made us even stronger as we got through all of it together," founder and owner Ashley Acers said.

Finally, some found an anchor in the very core of what matters most to them. "As a parent, I have been anchored in what matters most to me, that my son is getting the most valuable education in play and exploration surrounded by community and love," said Jess Durrett, who sends her son to Muck and Wonder Farm School. The school's director, Jenna Maggard, also found an anchor in "what our program is about, how to live our lives more purposefully and with intention."

"In many ways stripping away what was predictable left us with our shared values, strong culture, trusting colleagues, and our appreciation for one another," said Andrea Sisbarro, school director at Boulder Journey School. Executive director Alison Maher found herself and the school anchored in their style of "networking and connecting with schools around the world."

COVID prompted us to look within, calling upon the very best of ourselves so we could face daunting challenges and adversity. In the process we not only navigated through difficulty but grew stronger, dramatically improving the quality of our programs and our own characters. Our schools got better, and so did we.

Sculptor

Within adversity, some of us experienced a sculpting, a reshaping of our schools and even of ourselves. In losing so much, we came ever closer to our core, finding possibility in that process.

My own school, Discovery Village Childcare and Preschool, experienced COVID primarily as a sculptor. During the darkest of days, when we had only a tiny number of students attending, when we faced numerous COVID-19 cases and quarantines, and when staffing shortages stretched us to our limits, we found strength by chipping away everything that was not essential. We did it not by repeating the narrative of who we had been before—a place offering children from six weeks to five years the care of a village, the creativity of an art studio, and the discovery of a science lab. We still love that version of ourselves, and it remains central to who we are. Yet during the pandemic, we needed to rely far more strongly on other parts of ourselves, parts we hadn't even fully realized existed, parts we discovered only when we chiseled away the extraneous pieces.

We sculpted the way we teach, by stepping back and observing. Typically we would observe our students, seeking to understand their interests. We would then create learning experiences stemming from the activities and materials that spark their curiosity. But now, instead of observing only our students, we were also observing ourselves, seeking to understand the qualities of character we intuitively called upon and the environment we were creating. From there, we were able to strengthen and redesign our program.

Find Your Spark

Design a spark board.

This can be on a wall, a poster board, a bulletin board, or any other surface you choose. Take out sticky notes and write challenges you face. Post them on your spark board.

Now, reflect on those challenges, those sparks, that ignite you and fuel your momentum for reaching your goals.

Are there catalysts? Accelerators? Anchors? Sculptors?

Choose at least one spark. Or determine whether a spark has chosen you. This happens when a challenge presents itself that you must address.

Lean in close to your spark. Plan ways you will allow it to propel you forward.

Three qualities emerged for me as core in our process of sculpting: calm equanimity, playful possibility, and radical openness. Never in more than twenty years of serving as a values-driven educational leader had I chosen those qualities as my core values. I hadn't even considered them as options. Yet I found in those frightening, intense days that what I intuitively sought to create was a place of playful calm in which physical safety and social-emotional wellness are prioritized. I wanted to share fully and freely whatever information I had, good or bad, with my leadership team, my staff, and parents in my school. Having realized what I was aiming for, through sculpting away the rest, I intentionally nurtured those qualities so I could design the environment I believed my students and families needed most at the time.

Others engaged in similar processes of "uncovering" to arrive at what they and their communities needed most. "Spending more time alone in our homes led to a lot of self-reflection, peeling back the layers of what is really true for teaching communities," reflected Jenna Maggard. "Families felt so much more present." In that environment of adversity and presence, Jenna made intentional choices as a leader about what to let go of and what to build upon. She deliberately sculpted her school environment as well as her own leadership, actively designing the way she wanted to show up for her students and for her community.

Throughout our organizations we realized there were activities, programs, and even people we needed to release so we could move forward. "Shaving away the extras, connecting deeply to what matters most, and shedding members of the community who are not a right fit" helped Randolph School move ever closer to what Josh Kaplan describes as his aspirational vision of what school can be. Karen Eilersen and Jessica Holder of Discovery Child Care Centre found their essence, creating forest education training, shifting to a fully plant-based menu, and continually focusing on ways to more fully live their values. For Shawna Thompson, shedding relationships was far more personal. During the months of the pandemic, she and her husband separated. Shawna gained perspective and heightened focus on designing both the school and the life she wants for herself, her own children, and her students.

We can actively choose not to go back to the time before we knew how very capable we are.

Having experienced so much, we can actively decide to embrace our experiences as a way to continue to adapt and thrive, not because we have to, but because we choose to.

9

Letting Go to Move Forward

The beginning of the 2021–2022 academic year brought a heightened experience of adversity. Following a brief respite when we thought vaccines would make a massive impact in stemming the virus, the highly contagious Delta variant surged. Despite the availability of vaccines, not all who were eligible chose to be vaccinated, and children under twelve were not yet eligible. As in the beginning days of the pandemic, the most prevalent stories we were hearing in the field were of adversity and lack. After well over a year of pandemic, we heard many speaking of exhaustion and burnout. There was also controversy, rage, and even threats of violence against school board members in some districts by people who disagreed with their COVID policies and protocols, particularly the expectation that people mask and get vaccinated. And yet, similar to the way it had been during the earliest days of the pandemic, there was another story emerging, a quieter story, one of hope, resilience, and ongoing improvement. Persevering on this journey of transformation that we were on, despite the many challenges, required much effort. It also required release. There were things we needed to let go of. Some of what we had to let go of would be easy. Other parts would be far more challenging. But throughout the process, assessing what needed to go would be freeing.

Things many of us looked to let go of included what you think things should be; what is no longer working; distractions; the need for control; judging ourselves; comparisons with others; standardization; the distinction between school and home, learning and life; and the way things have always been.

Letting Go of What You Think Things Should Be

"I let go of perceptions, let go of what I thought was expected of me. I let go of the idea that teaching has to be a certain way," said teacher Mary Roux Train, cofounder of Windsor Hill Primary School, describing her move to open a pod and then a microschool. The process wasn't easy. "What is real and true comes through difficult situations. Learning at its best isn't easy. If we only did easy we wouldn't learn. We need to believe in ourselves. To do that you have to let go of what you think things should be."

Mary, energized and enthusiastic about the next stage in her journey, expressed hope that more educators would "step out of what they do and what they think they believe." She acknowledged that the process of doing so is challenging. "Maybe you don't feel like stepping out or trying something new. That is a choice. Our entire lives are a choice." Mary gets it. She said that before the pandemic, "I never thought about doing this. I've pulled together dreams I never even knew were there."

Letting Go of What Is No Longer Working

At Discovery Village, I adopted a saying throughout the pandemic: *It will work until it doesn't.* The challenges were coming at a dizzying pace. So were the solutions. What faced us one month, one week, one day, sometimes even one hour was not necessarily what would face us the next. We needed to detach from solutions that no longer worked. We needed to stop trying to solve the problems of yesterday when facing the problems of today.

Letting go was challenging because we were so proud of what we were implementing. Yet we intentionally disciplined ourselves not to become too attached to a solution or to attach our identities too closely to solving any one problem. By embracing the notion that the things we were doing would not work forever, we could shift course as challenges arose. We were able to maintain the sense of calm equanimity, playful possibility, and radical openness that together became our North Star through the most challenging of times.

Letting Go of Distractions

"If not for the pandemic, I don't think we would have made the progress we did. We didn't have the stresses and distractions of other times," said Cecilia Cruz Brooks, a member of My Reflection Matters Village. Letting go of their packed schedules released Cecilia's children to engage more fully in what they truly wanted to do. Both Cecilia and her children are now much more comfortable dropping out of activities that do not serve their needs. "Before I just kept trying. Not just me, also the kids. We kept up with things because we committed to them and thought we had to follow through," Cecilia shared. "Now I will not be afraid to say no, change things up. It's not giving up. It's just saying this approach didn't work."

Dominique DjeDje, another member of My Reflection Matters Village, has also become far more discerning about the activities she chooses. "I don't want any part of returning to the rat race. I want to focus my energy on what I care about."

Letting Go of the Need for Control and Letting Go of Judging Ourselves

"So much was about having faith and keeping the bigger picture in mind. We had to let go of the need for control," said Ilana Friedman, director and lead teacher of Beacon Hebrew Alliance Preschool. Alongside letting go of the need for control, many of us recognized the need for greater self-acceptance. "I let go of judging myself," Ilana said.

Committed to play-based learning, Ilana used the skills that emerge through play to navigate through the many challenges she faced as a leader. "We had to play so much with the options. We planned and became immersed in a rich curricular flow," she said. Then, with a COVID-19 exposure, community members went into quarantine and the school needed to shift to remote learning. "We were discovering possibilities we didn't notice before. It took obstacles to discover opportunities and resources all around us."

Letting Go of Comparisons with Others

"Sometimes you can't help but compare your kids to other kids their age," said Chemay Morales-James, founder of My Reflection Matters Village. Parents understand children learn at different rates, yet the language of schoolishness and expectations of what is supposed to be are difficult to escape. To support one another on the journey of letting go of comparisons, adults in My Reflection Matters Village often speak about ways they are holding on to traditional models of schooling as well as comparisons with others, intentionally helping one another to let go of these limiting perspectives.

Letting Go of Standardization

"The constant push for academics is not working for our kids," said Kaitlin Coppola, founder of Emergent Expressions. It has been important to her to let go of performance standards. As Kaitlin was trained as a public school teacher, even *stating* that she is letting go of performance standards is frightening for her. Setting herself free from expectations of what children should accomplish at each grade level has been a challenge. Yet she believes that when kids are allowed to reclaim their own learning pace, direct their learning, and pursue their interests, great changes will happen in society. "We have been trained with the belief that we need to consume more and more knowledge," Kaitlin said. "Yet when we let go of the need to consume, we will be able to be present, in our bodies and in our world, making choices that will benefit ourselves and one another."

Letting Go of the Distinction between School and Home, Learning and Life

"For a long time I tried to decompartmentalize," explained Chemay, keeping school and home separate. Yet in time she accepted that "in decolonized learning, the lines are blurry. Parents are educators, and educators take on parental roles. It is important to stop boxing in the roles as entirely separate. They are meant to mesh together." In self-directed learning there has been a paradigm shift. Unlike traditional teachers, who control the narrative of education, in self-directed learning educators function as facilitators and guides.

In the early weeks of remote learning, Dominique DjeDje began by, in her words, "re-creating school at home." Yet the desks she set up for her children stood empty as they chose to learn while lying on the floor, sitting at the table, or walking up and down the stairs. Observing her children "reimagining how learning can look," Dominique took note. "Learning can happen in a lot of ways. It does not need to be at wooden desks, sitting upright."

When Dominique's daughter became interested in building a dollhouse, Dominique explained that "she didn't take a class to learn how to build a dollhouse. She just started." Dominique wondered aloud why so many embrace self-learning for hobbies yet not for school. "Why can't we own our learning, learn in our own way?" she asked. "We are moving from the information age to the experiential age. More and more companies don't want degrees. They want skills. That's what the village is all about for children and for me. It's all about trust, trusting yourself, trusting your child."

"For us there is no difference between school and home because I'm still learning," My Reflection Matters Village member Tamsyn Ambler said. "My education is not complete," Cecilia Cruz Brooks concurred. In the village "everyone is co-learning, and nobody, neither child nor adult, is made to feel ashamed for not knowing something," Cecilia said. "Kids see human beings being themselves in a healthy way."

Letting Go of the Way Things Have Always Been

Starting a new school with a unique approach was a "scary leap of faith," said Maria Ferrari, founder of Acton Academy Silicon Valley. It took courage to try to do things a different way and faith that "we won't mess up our children." Still, Maria is proud of letting go of the current school model and its emphasis on "compliance, not deviating, being told what to do, memorizing material, and moving on," she said. "Letting go of a system that doesn't trust kids to want to learn without grades as a measurement of success has opened space for an environment in which kids love to learn." Maria is proud of creating a space allowing children to direct their own learning, emphasizing critical thinking and problem solving.

Cassandra Clausen, founder of the Open School, also described the importance of letting go of the way things have always been. "This year has

Letting Go

Close your eyes. Imagine yourself on a beach at night. A bonfire is burning. You are surrounded by people you care about and who care about you.

Set an intention for something you want to accomplish. Imagine it coming into being. Share with those around you what has occurred, as if it has already happened.

Now to make that happen, imagine at least one thing you must release, letting go of it to move forward. Write it on a piece of paper and throw it into that fire.

Return to this activity as often as you like.

been a trial by fire," she said, following up with a question: "Can we shift our mindset or will we remain stuck in what we have always been doing?" Cassandra said she believes the stakes are high. "We can expect more pandemics and more severe weather events." Given that, she asked, "Can we get away from a place of fear and anxiety? How do we prepare in a hopeful way? What creative resources can we utilize as educators preparing for the future with a really creative mindset instead of a fear- and constraint-based mindset?" The answers remain to be seen, or rather, actively designed. For Cassandra, at least one thing is certain. To get to where our children need us to be, we will need to open our hearts and minds to the possible, letting go of a reliance on the way things have always been.

Having identified sparks and released what no longer serves, you are ready not only to navigate through whatever challenge you face but also to get better. The REVABILITIES™ framework can serve as a guide and foundation. Again, the twelve pillars are

R: relationships and responsiveness

E: experiences and environment

V: vision and values

A: adversity and authenticity

B: budget and busy-ness (resources of money and time)

ILITIES: abilities and possibilities

As you read the following chapters, delving into each of the twelve REVABILITIES™ pillars, consider ways you might be standing at a founding moment. What possibilities do you see for yourself and your career? What are the significant challenges you see our world facing that you believe education can address? For Maria Montessori it was independence and peace. For Rudolf Steiner it was revitalization. For Loris Malaguzzi it was standing strong against oppression, injustice, and inequity. What is it that you stand for? And how do you see yourself making a contribution to bring about the world you seek?

Relationships and Responsiveness

In a world facing so many crises and so much pain, we adapted. We became ever more responsive to the emerging and shifting needs of the children, families, and communities we serve. Through our relationships with one another, we found strength and possibility we had not even known existed.

We nurtured relationships and demonstrated responsiveness in a variety of ways, including being present, building trust, strengthening professional cultures, connecting authentically, prioritizing self-care, and embracing the possibility of being part of something bigger than ourselves.

Being Present

"We were nervous and scared. It wasn't easy to wake up every morning and see the world falling apart. But we could remain together, come through together," said Karina Wyllie, owner of Koala Park Daycare. Her words articulately conveyed what so many of us experienced during those early days of the pandemic. "We were just busy, going, going, going, which allowed us to forget a little bit about how scared we were, our own personal worries, and focus on serving others." Listening to Karina, I thought back to my own experience of the earliest days of the pandemic. For me, too, the constant motion of those early days allowed me to numb thoughts of how terrified I was.

In time we settled into a new reality, a new rhythm of life. "The piece that remained the same for us, on a very deep level," said Cori Berg, executive director of Hope Day School, "is that the most important thing to us is not philosophy, not curriculum, not equipment. It is person-to-person connection. There is a lot we can get through: masks, rough times with staffing, and frustrations with each other. We are able to have fun because we are able to connect."

Communities thrived as their leaders demonstrated responsiveness and flexibility. "We became the constant for families," said Rachel Happel, K–12 director at Temple Beth Shalom. She and her colleagues redefined what being present and highly responsive can mean, entirely reimagining learning opportunities for their community. Jenna Maggard, director of Muck and Wonder Farm School, transformed the organization from a parent-participation preschool into a nature program for school-age children because it was what families in her community needed most.

Members of school communities grew increasingly responsive to one another. "The parent community became much more involved. They strengthened and sustained a sense of community with each other and the school, aligned in the values of keeping the school open and safe, both physically and emotionally. The year has been all about bringing comfort to each other," said Stacey Seltzer, cofounder of Hudson Lab School.

Windsor Hill's cofounder Mary Roux Train gained strength through connections with the children she taught and their families. "Without the relationships with those in my pod, I would have needed mental health support," she said. "We call ourselves the pod family."

At Beacon Hebrew Alliance Preschool, a far stronger sense of interdependence between families and staff emerged. "Far more of a collaborative dialogue has gone into constructing this particular epic year," director and lead teacher Ilana Friedman said of the 2020–2021 school year. The range of challenges was immense, and in facing them together, members of the community developed a lot more compassion for one another. Parents stepped in to assist, clearing their schedules to be present as needed with tremendous generosity. Through it all, trust grew, and the community found that together, members were able to withstand enormous adversity.

Karina Wyllie emphasized how she became more open to personal conversations with her staff. "Everyone was under so much stress, and you had to show them you care." One staff member had lost her dad to COVID-19 right before Karina hired her. The experience highlighted to Karina the importance of opening herself to staff and making space for staff to open themselves up to her.

Students flourished when their teachers were highly responsive. "COVID showed me how essential it is to first connect, and only then start teaching," relayed Josiane Sawaya, a teacher in the Santa Clara Unified School District. Although not physically together with her students, Josiane was highly present and responsive, nurturing strong relationships. "When you make a connection, call a child's name or spotlight a child and see how they smile, it makes a difference. Online or in person, you need to connect," she asserted. "If you don't make a connection, you become a YouTuber, not a teacher." She showered love not only on children in her program but also on parents. "We would cry together, laugh together, and support each other," she said. "Helping parents is helping kids indirectly. To care for kids, it's important to start with parents. The parents rely on us more."

Virtual communities thrived, with people staying emotionally present for one another and responsive to each other's needs, even when physically distanced. "Virtual relationships are real relationships, not fly-by relationships," shared Chemay Morales-James, founder of My Reflection Matters Village. "Relationships are the most impactful and largest benefit" of participation in the village.

In the end, many of us were incredibly proud of what we had accomplished together and of who we had become in the process. "Like facing trauma in childhood, later on it feels like we are on a different planet," relayed Josiane. "Yet there are joyful moments during the hard times. Later I will wonder whether I really lived through this. There were so many instances I thought there was no way I could do it. Yet I am alive—not only alive, I am supporting other people. That is a huge gift."

We came to hold a far greater appreciation for health, for life, and for one another. "You tell people you love them more," said Kaye Boehning, director of Tomorrow's Promise. "With a sense of the fragility of life, you let people know you care." Josiane concurred, reflecting emotionally on things she will miss from the frightening, turbulent months of the pandemic. "We will miss family breakfasts, lunches, and dinners together, family walks. I will miss the first group of kids I taught during the pandemic, from March to June. I will always remember their faces. They will always be in my mind and in my heart."

With her grounding in love, Karina articulated what so many of us felt: "You have to be able to live with your heart open and connect on a deeper level, a human level. Relationships can break you if they are not healthy, if you are not allowing yourself to love and let love in. Love, connection, and relationships are interconnected. When you have that in life, everything else will come to you. You could be poor financially but lead a very wealthy life."

Building Trust

"We have much braver spaces now," asserted Karen Eilersen, founder and owner of Discovery Child Care Centre. She brought her faculty together for a month prior to reopening. "We had been apart for six months, with only superficial checking in. We were able to really be together with intention," she said. With the focused time on building trust within her team, Karen brought to life a long-held, previously aspirational culture of safety in disagreeing. "In that month together, learning and planning without children present, we developed more trusting and open relationships. It was transformational."

"Trusting myself and building a mindset of upleveling through trusting my amazing team" has been central to the success at Building Blocks Preschool, owner Suzanne Gabli shared. This trust is connected to living in gratitude. Suzanne said she is proud that her team "knows who they are. I can trust them." The trust began with Suzanne herself. "When I trust myself, I can trust them more. When you doubt yourself, you doubt everyone else. It sounds simple, yet it requires daily practice. You don't just do this once. You have to live it."

"You just need to get resourceful," Karina said. "Look inside of you. Trust in the people around you. Trust in your team." This includes supporting staff emotionally as well as showing them appreciation. "My job is to be there for them; to motivate, train, and show them the way; tell them I believe in them; let them know they can do this so that hopefully they can believe in themselves."

Karina extends her emphasis on trust to families in her program. "Our business is based on trust," she said. "Especially in this type of industry, people have to trust you. If not, at the first instance that they see or hear something they don't like, they will be out the door. Our families last. The majority stay and come back with their second and third child. They feel the love. We put a lot of love and effort into everything we do."

Recognizing the vital importance of trust, Cate Han and Stacey Seltzer planned professional learning on the topic. They brought in a training program "on building trust in groups, creating a forum allowing people to be themselves, to be authentic with one another," Stacey shared. Cassandra Clausen, founder of the Open School, similarly brought in professional training for her team with a program guiding them to dive deeper into their relationships with one another, emphasizing ways of working through conflict.

Sara Lev, a transitional kindergarten teacher at Larchmont Charter School, flourished with the trust placed in her by her school's administration. "So much trust was put in us as early childhood teachers to know how kids learn best. Our administration trusted us to know students and families and what is best for them," she said.

Strengthening Professional Cultures

"We are more like family than two teachers on a team," Josiane Sawaya of the Santa Clara Unified School District said of her coteacher. Her sentiment was shared widely. Those who navigated through adversity and got better said they embraced the support of others. "In the beginning I didn't want to ask for help or rely on anyone else. Yet we need to rely on relationships and connections that pull us up," Josiane said.

"Nobody [at Boulder Journey School] is going to take colleagues for granted," said school director Andrea Sisbarro. "We realize how interdependent we are." Andrea said she also appreciates her relationships with other local Boulder County educators. The professionals conferred frequently as they sought to navigate through the decision of remaining open or closing and then reopening during the pandemic. "It was reassuring to know that we would figure this out together," she said.

Cassandra Clausen had long appreciated her monthly meetings with executive directors of local nonprofits. The group had been meeting in person pre-pandemic and seamlessly shifted sessions to a remote venue. "The group was a lifeline," Cassandra said. Through collaboration with her colleagues and a professional coach provided by the group, Cassandra reframed her approach, shifting her democratic school model to a remote learning environment.

Collegial relationships flourished over great geographic distances. Cate Han and Stacey Seltzer received tremendous support from the Innovative Schools Cooperative, a group of leaders serving microschools throughout the country. Pre-pandemic, they would see these peers once a year at a conference. During the pandemic they connected far more regularly. Joy Anderson and members of Preschool All Stars Membership could have felt paralyzed when schools throughout the country went remote. But Joy brought the membership together, confident they could figure out how to move forward. They shifted from running in-person preschools to online preschools in just seven days. Joy's pride in her members shone through as she emotionally talked about the ways in which they have become "a true sisterhood, a community."

Some nurtured new collegial relationships. Pedagogical leader Jessica Holder of Discovery Child Care Centre reached out to other early childhood programs in similar contexts to share ideas and gain inspiration. Before COVID she hadn't realized how open other educators are to sharing. The interactions have revealed ways of making a difference within a global educational community in which multiple voices are far more impactful than any of us can be on our own.

Connecting Authentically

In the rawness of this incredibly challenging time, "people showed up as their authentic selves," said Lauren Weatherly, partner school program director at Boulder Journey School. "There were no facades. There was no time to think about facades." The "real human desire to connect" shone through, as did a passionate commitment to serving children and families, she said. Boulder Journey School's virtual dialogues with educators were "consistently healing, productive, and positive," Lauren said. "The connections extended to raw, authentic connections among teachers in ways not typical of work spaces. It was really freeing."

Previous homeschool environments in which Cecilia Cruz Brooks had participated as a member were "very white-centered spaces, with little or no mindfulness culturally." In those environments Cecilia felt isolated and lonely. She could not fully connect because of "different ways to speak, different ways to do things, and even for looking 'exotic.'" Finding My Reflection Matters changed everything for her. "I love how the kids are always around, part of meetings, watching us in community, talking or listening, in such a liberated way in this decolonized, liberated space. I've never before been in a space like this. It is the first time I am experiencing a village."

Member Dominique DjeDje spoke of the depth of conversations in the village with appreciation. There is a ritual in which members invite one another to speak about one or more moments that matter: a moment of schoolishness, a moment of liberation, and a moment of self-love. "It's a beautiful, more authentic way of sharing," Dominique said. "It's so specific to people who are homeschooling, unschooling, or self-directed. And it's not just educational. It's how we parent and how we live life. It flows organically. That's what I've observed. I've made closer friends in a shorter time than ever before."

Whether virtually, in physical communities, or in some combination, at the heart of My Reflection Matters Village is a deep grounding in relationships. "We are engaged in a parenting shift," Chemay Morales-James said. "It's hard to be in community in the larger society where most don't understand our approach to parenting and learning. . . . In the village we feel a reprieve. It feels so good to be here, take a weight off our shoulders and relax a little bit."

Prioritizing Self-Care

"Self-care was already a buzzword before COVID," Dominique stated. In that pre-COVID world, she had thought of self-care as going to the spa and getting a manicure and pedicure. While asserting there is nothing wrong with that, today her views are far more expansive. To Dominique, self-care includes time focused inward through meditation, mindfulness, breathing, and time in nature. It also includes political activism. "During COVID I had time to read, delve deeper, and reimagine activism." Through her learning, Dominique encountered new perspectives. She became inspired by the work of writer Audre Lorde, who famously declared self-care to be an act of political warfare. "Self-care for Black women has been countercultural," Dominique said. "Others had expected us to be working/slaving." She has become ever more appreciative of her own freedom. "Self-care for me is now about how to unapologetically, vocally focus on care for myself and my family and encouraging friends" to do so as well.

For village member Tamsyn Ambler, self-care is, at the very least, slowing down. "We value time in a different way. We are so much more aware of each other's self-care. It's OK not to check email for a few days, not to be plugged in. It's OK not to be at every meeting, OK to be in a bad mood, OK to be who you are."

A self-care routine has long been vital to Karina Wyllie. This includes exercising, eating healthfully, hydrating well, and following a daily morning routine of journaling and meditation. "I've been doing this for years, and it does help," she explained. These practices helped her navigate through the most challenging days. Relationships have also long been central to Karina's self-care routine and continued to be so throughout the pandemic. "Connection, loving connections, include making sure to touch base with family and having virtual drinks with friends. At the day care, in the beginning when we were virtual, it was very important to stay connected with the kids and families."

Through the months of the pandemic, the leadership team at Boulder Journey School became far more intentional about self-care. Their initial impulse was to give generously to the field, organizing virtual dialogues that brought together educators from around the world. They hadn't realized how much they would receive through these connections. In every virtual dialogue, part of the conversation focused on how educators were "taking care of ourselves, being cared for, and caring for our community," said Lauren Weatherly.

Some have brought self-care intentionally to their schools. Sara Lev begins every day with either meditation, yoga, or exercise for herself. She shares these practices with her students, helping them to develop a tool kit to regulate their emotions. In addition to teaching her students mindfulness, breathing techniques, and yoga, Sara offers them the gift of time and space to be themselves. Her classroom features a peace corner where students can retreat as they need to do so. There they can practice the tools of self-regulation Sara has taught or simply take a moment to decompress. The time, space, and tools for self-care are so vital to Sara that when her school shifted to remote learning, one of the first activities she did with her students was support them to create a peace corner at home.

In leading her school through the challenges and adversity of the pandemic, Cori Berg learned a vital lesson. "I can't just give of myself. There also needs to be a role for others in helping to care for me as the leader. We all need to work to take care of each other. One person can't do it all." Giving grace and forgiveness expansively, Cori expects her teachers to be compassionate as well, with each other, with parents, and with Cori herself. At a time when all of us were under tremendous stress, Cori modeled through her actions and clarified through her words her expectation that care for all be central. "The lesson of the pandemic," she asserted, "is how to be a good human."

For Kaitlin Coppola of Emergent Expressions, self-care has been a quest to be her best self. To do that, she is intentional about modeling emotional awareness to her students. "When teaching in public school, I left myself at the door. Here I have the freedom to be both Kaitlin and a teacher." She coaches parents to do the same. Parents have good days and bad. Kaitlin advises encouraging children to use a tablet or do something else they enjoy, without guilt, when parents need some time to care for themselves. "If your adult cup is empty, if you are stressed and overwhelmed, you can't be patient with children," she asserted. All parents, and perhaps particularly parents who homeschool, need to be able to give themselves the grace and the space to be human and regroup when under pressure so that they can return and give the best of themselves to their children. Teachers need the same.

Embracing the Possibility of Being Part of Something Bigger Than Ourselves

"Little tiny sparks on their own can't light things on fire; enough of these sparks can light a fire. Amazing things will happen," asserted Jessica Holder. "There is a realization that there is a reckoning that needs to happen."

"Before the pandemic, I was more pessimistic," she reflected. "I had the feeling I didn't have the ability to make a difference. I feel differently now. I have had so many conversations with professionals who want to think differently." These conversations are, in part, the result of the seamless incorporation of video conferencing into our daily lives. The ubiquity of the technology led many, Jessica included, to become far more adept at nurturing meaningful relationships remotely. "I have a new level of vulnerability. A year ago I never thought I could have real, vulnerable conversations over Zoom," she said.

"I began reading the stories of others in this book. I don't even know them yet and I already feel a connection," she said. She grew into seeing herself as part of a global community of people seeking to make an impact, to get better. Jessica reflected on how other centers she knew were "just surviving, just getting through the days. We leaned in with openness to be a different way." She said she sees the pandemic as a beginning of sorts. "I think more people are realizing the possibility of being part of something bigger."

11

Experiences and Environment

"The energy and vibe at our school feels happier and more stable," shared Jessica Holder, pedagogical leader at Discovery Child Care Centre. "It is an energy-giving environment. There is an increase in risk-taking among teachers. We are more willing to share ideas outside the norm. People have come to feel happier." Her words brought me great joy. I felt them myself at Discovery Village. Yes, educators worldwide faced so many challenges, and yes there were so many times we were overwhelmed and exhausted. We understood the grief and pain in the world around us, and we did not take our health or ability to serve those in our care for granted. Still, not always, but often, we felt happier.

I wondered how, in times of stress and despair, we were finding joy. I found my answer in the experiences we were offering and the environments we were designing. Long passionate about experiential learning, I found the play- and project-based methodology my school embraces resonated ever more powerfully for me during the dark and uncertain early days of the pandemic. Yet even as the significance of experiential learning grew, I recognized my school needed something more, something different. I began focusing as much on environment as on experience, as much on "being" as on "doing."

I remember distinctly the moment I realized we would need to emphasize not only experience, long central to my vision for learning, but also environment. It was during morning drop-off, right after we had closed for just eight days, at the very beginning of our experience of the pandemic. Most child care centers that remained open were requiring parents to drop their children off at the door. I tried that in the beginning. Yet, very early on, a mom arrived with her toddler and at the door both burst into tears. There was so much stress, and they needed more time to ease into the day. "You come in," I asserted, making the decision on the spot that we would be a place that is intentional about tending to the emotional as well as physical safety of our children and, to the extent that we could, their parents as well. We would find ways to safely connect even while we were required to physically isolate. The phrase *haven of hope* came to my mind, and I set out from that moment to nurture experiences and an environment that would immerse children, parents, and staff in hopeful possibility.

In emphasizing both experience and environment we focused on a number of goals, including bringing our best passions and our best selves to our work; simplifying our priorities; embracing adaptability; and revamping our messaging.

Bringing Our Best Passions and Our Best Selves to Our Work

We slowed down, intentionally focusing not only on what we do but also on who we are, becoming far more present for our children as well as for each other. Navigating through the pandemic "transformed the entire staff, fundamentally changing the way we teach," shared Randolph School director Josh Kaplan. Teachers increasingly "bring their best passions and their best selves," he explained. Long focused on connection to the planet and the natural environment, staff and students at Randolph developed a much deeper relationship with the land and with biodiversity in the natural world. They also have a much stronger embrace of diversity among individuals within and beyond the community. "I had no idea how much better Randolph could be," he said.

Simplifying Our Priorities

"We simplified our priorities," said Suzanne Gabli, owner of Building Blocks Preschool. Suzanne and her team focused on creating an environment in which students and staff alike know they are loved for who they are. "What is vital is not getting through a lesson plan," no matter how expertly crafted, Suzanne said. Instead what matters is an environment in which educators are fully present with the children.

Embracing Adaptability

Slowing down helped educators become increasingly adaptable, providing increasingly meaningful experiences and an environment of calm even as demand for change came at breakneck speed. "Sometimes you have to choose a solution even if you don't have all the information you wish you had," said Cori Berg, executive director of Hope Day School. "You may shift course, but that doesn't mean you were wrong. It's a sign that you are willing to look at other factors, take in knowledge, and adjust." In the past, Cori and her staff would become far more distressed when decisions needed to be changed. They now understand "that's how life is; that's how organizations are," she said.

While this openness to adapting improved our schools, it also helped us become ever better versions of ourselves. "The staff that have been with us all along or most of the way have much greater resilience in the day-to-day, small, uncomfortable moments we have with each other," Cori said. Additionally, "we understand we all have limits." Together, she and her team have emerged as a more caring community, prepared to tackle new challenges as they emerge.

The speed at which events were happening, combined with openness and adaptability, led many of us to make decisions we would not have previously considered in order to be as responsive as possible to the needs of those we serve. "We transformed from education-based support for children to a community space in which parents come together, feel a sense of belonging, and together talk out challenges," said Dominique DjeDje, a member of My Reflection Matters Village. "We have transformed, evolved." As communities shifted, many became far more comfortable with finding people aligned with their visions and with letting go of people not aligned who leave or choose not to join. "My Reflection Matters Village is not for everyone, but nobody's program should be for everyone," member Tamsyn Ambler asserted. Numerous programs experienced the same. Many families were joining our programs, and we were filling up. Some were leaving, no longer aligned with who we were becoming. While the process was often heartrending, it was at the same time healthy. Many of us had navigated through enormous challenges by being ever more true to the essence of who we are.

Revamping Our Messaging

Recognizing the changes in ourselves, in the experiences we offer and the environment we created, some found that the words we used to describe ourselves had not kept pace with our transformations. Center owner Karina Wyllie conveyed a sentiment that a number of us experienced, sharing that Koala Park Daycare's "verbiage and message doesn't fully describe us and who we really are." So she embarked on a process of revamping her messaging. As part of that process, she conducted a competitive analysis, seeking to understand how Koala Park compared to other child care programs in her area. What she found surprised her. "Everybody looks the same," Karina said she discovered. "A lot of places tell parents what they want to hear. We are different."

Celebrating Koala Park's uniqueness, Karina looked inward, determined to even more clearly articulate and more intentionally bring to life the Koala Park Daycare difference. Reviewing the high level of service, the impactful experiences, and the nurturing environment she offers, she set a course forward, dedicated to finding ways to further increase quality and impact. She was by no means alone. Many of us were intentionally reviewing and clarifying our messaging to reflect more accurately who we have become, and then setting out to improve on what uniquely distinguishes us.

12

Vision and Values

In the early days of the pandemic, Jessica Holder, pedagogical leader of Discovery Child Care Centre, searched online for "how to be a leader during a pandemic." There were no results. While writing this section in May 2021, I also looked up "how to be a leader during a pandemic." So much had changed. At the point I searched, I was rewarded with millions of results. We have learned so much. Still, as Jessica's early query powerfully attests, there were critical moments when there were no outside sources of wisdom to be found and we had to look within. We found our way forward by getting clear on what matters most, finding the solutions to challenges from within our vision and our values, and seeing the possibility for a massive reset.

Getting Clear on What Matters Most

Like many schools and businesses, prior to COVID, Discovery Child Care Centre had a written list of core values and a strategic plan. "It was a piece of paper on the wall that we had for the sake of having. COVID has brought our values to life," Jessica explained. She and founder and owner Karen Eilersen met with faculty and engaged in deep conversations.

"We had to get really clear on our values," Jessica said. This included not only the school's stated values but also the deeply held values of each staff member. Together, the staff worked to weave the values of individual team members together. From there, they brought their vision and their values into behaviors they wanted to see in the school. They made decisions, large and small, by grounding themselves in those priorities. Jessica described the process as being so special that it was difficult to come up with a word to describe it. The closest she came was to call it *magical*.

Some schools immediately knew the course of action they needed to take. For example, central to the very identity of Tomorrow's Promise is, as articulated by director Kaye Boehning, the school's commitment to "staying open, being present for families." When the pandemic hit, Kaye knew "we had to live our values." Her families, the vast majority of whom are essential workers, relied on her school to remain open.

For Nelum Walpola, directress of White Dove Montessori, what mattered most was maintaining respect for her students. Never before adept with technology, Nelum adapted to online learning. Even in a remote environment, she found ways to convey her deep respect for children and her commitment to engaging, hands-on learning, central to the Montessori approach she has long valued.

For My Reflection Matters Village member Dominique DjeDje, COVID sparked reflection about what she valued most, causing her to look at many things in different ways. At the beginning of the pandemic, Dominique shut down her business as a professional organizer. Although her family has substantially less income, Dominique has been grateful for the freedom her decision to pause has afforded her. She joined My Reflection Matters Village, where she has found a community of individuals who share her values of peaceful, decolonized parenting and treating all humans, including children, with respect and care. Through her active engagement in the village, she has become much more confident and assured in her embrace of these values.

Dominique attributes much of the value-rich experience within the My Reflection Matters Village to the clarity that founder Chemay Morales-James infuses. This includes what the village is and whom it's for, as well as what the village does not support and does not believe in. While inclusive, for example embracing Dominique's choice to send her daughters to school, there still is exclusivity based on core values. The conviction that there is no one definition of liberation is central to My Reflection Matters Village's approach. Still, for Chemay, the core of liberation-centered learning is that children are seen as equal in partnership with parents. "It's hard to say you believe in liberation-centered learning if kids do not have any say. There is a shift in the hierarchy of adults and kids, a parenting lifestyle."

For Chemay this approach celebrates "reconnecting with ancestral ways of teaching and learning" and is deeply grounded in Afro-Indigenous roots. Chemay hearkens back to a time in which children learned through doing and through storytelling: "Self-directed education is ancestral, not new, not revolutionary—it is intergenerational learning by doing." The value of connecting to her Afro-Indigenous spiritual heritage, formed in the village, has been transformative for member Cecilia Cruz Brooks. Although raised by an Afro-Latino father and an Indigenous Mexican mother, while growing up Cecilia experienced a painful generational disconnect from the spirituality of her ancestors. Reconnecting with these practices has changed the way she feels both physically and emotionally. By embracing life in a decolonized way, Cecilia has been able to be unapologetically herself while embracing nature as a pathway to connect with her heritage and her spirituality. Seeing her children's awareness of how humans affect the environment brings Cecilia hope for the future.

Finding the Solutions to Challenges from Within Our Vision and Our Values

"I'm passionate about what I'm doing," shared Shawna Thompson, founding director of Sunbeam Nature School, "being a visionary, believing in this vision, believing this change in education has to happen. I am reaching out to try to influence others in addition to leading my own school. This mission feels like a calling, advocating for what is possible for children." Her sentiments reflect the perspectives of many who launched small, innovative programs.

"Values became the answer to the problem," said Cassandra Clausen, the founder of the Open School. She and her team went through a process of "shrinking back down to what is our core philosophy: autonomy within the context of a democratic community." In designing what was a whole new way of being, they dug into long-held democratic approaches, creating a virtual committee of students and faculty to plan virtual events. They delved into ways their school's approach could be translated into virtual spaces, creating an environment embracing student-created activities, projects, and programs.

Seeing the Possibility for a Massive Reset

Steering and shifting course in a system with more than 5,600 students and 1,000 staff members is a formidable challenge, but Bill Brennan, assistant superintendent for innovation and organizational development at the Farmingdale School District in New York, has set out to do just that. His efforts offer others a glimpse of what is possible on a larger scale. It isn't easy. Bill described the challenge of systemic change as "turning like an aircraft carrier when you need to turn like a Jet Ski."

In Bill's assessment, the shift to remote learning was "incredibly successful given the circumstances." That success ignited optimism or, in Bill's words, the "hopeful opportunity for a massive reset or reboot in what we believe to be our values system." It offered a moment for Bill to strive to "peel back our values" and participate in "meaningful revisioning of what we want to see."

By no means are all people in education, and specifically large districts, adopting the same perspective. Bill has found it to be "frustrating to see decisions to continue what we've just been doing." He advocates for local control of education and is weary of having to follow state and federal governmental legislation on education. Bill laments requirements "irrelevant to what kids need" broadly and the emphasis on standardized testing specifically. He has many ideas about ways other than testing for "kids to share their learning, open their eyes to what it means to experience learning."

"My role is really to lead bold conversations," Bill asserted. He's done that and more, advocating for spaces where students can themselves lead conversation on topics that matter to them. This has included conversations about equity, the Black Lives Matter movement, and ways to ensure that "*all* really means all." Bill spoke emphatically about the "need to fight and be relentless to give opportunities to kids."

The challenges of navigating through a pandemic brought Bill's district together as a community. "There is more patience and appreciation for what everyone does. I like to believe there is a greater level of empathy and compassion for each other." It wasn't easy, and there are distinctions among individual schools within the district. When there was a strong school culture in place, facing adversity together made the culture even stronger. When there was not a strong culture in place, it showed.

Bill imagines the possibility of a fundamental shift in how we view school. "Now we have the opportunity, having been through so much, to determine how to capture the moment and reboot the system as a broad community of learners. It is a moment of openness to change, a ripe opportunity to have bold ideas about what the future will look like."

13

Adversity and Authenticity

"If they took everything from us and just gave us an empty room with no windows, we would have found a way," Cori Berg, executive director of Hope Day School, emotionally relayed. "We would have told stories, sung songs, and run around."

I often think of Cori's words. So much was taken. And still we found a way to serve and improve. Or, more accurately, we found *many* ways to serve and improve. We transformed school cultures, started new schools, and even created new approaches to learning. We brought schools online and outside, opening up possibilities for global connection and for nature-based learning programs that could transcend the challenging months of pandemic.

"You have to live and learn," said Karina Wyllie, owner of Koala Park Daycare. "You always have to be open to change, learn new things, welcome challenges, welcome problems in your life. They will teach you because on the other side of problems is a better, bigger, smarter you. More than anything, what matters is who you become in the process."

We educators had faced adversity and had learned about ourselves, who we were and who we were capable of becoming. In the process, we drew into an authenticity we hadn't necessarily known we had. We relied "not on technical skills, but on character," Joy Anderson, owner of Preschool System and Preschool All Stars Membership reflected. "We need to prioritize character above skill set," Joy asserted.

Genuine, authentic connection to the values that would best help in our specific circumstances led me in particular to reconsider how we choose core values in our schools as well as how we infuse values into our learning experiences with our students. Prior to the pandemic, I spoke of Discovery Village as a place offering the care of a village, the creativity of an art studio, and the discovery of a science lab. Our core values, listed on our website, were caring, connecting, creating, and contributing. Those values, and that vision, still resonate for me. And yet, to navigate through the pandemic, they weren't enough.

Calm equanimity, playful possibility, and radical openness were the three values I called upon most during the challenging days of the pandemic. This was a huge surprise for me. I had never articulated those three values as core in the past. I hadn't even included them on lists of possible values. Yet what my center needed was calm, playfulness, and hope. In the most challenging moments, we needed truth. It wasn't the feel of an art studio or a science lab we needed most during those challenging days, as much as I love messy creativity with kids. We needed to feel like a haven of hope, a refuge from the chaos around us. That realization came intuitively, from being present and responsive to those around me.

Being authentic in times of adversity requires being open to surprising yourself by what emerges from within you and being responsive to what emerges from within those around you. Values will choose you, if you allow them to do so.

Core values matter. They tell part of the story of how we can stand out by what we stand for. Yet core values are not enough. We need a whole cabinet of values to draw from as we craft the experiences and the environments we seek for our communities and our families. In this way relationships and responsiveness, experiences and environment, vision and values, and adversity and authenticity are not separate at all. They combine in a magnificent tapestry that depicts our journey toward who we are becoming.

As you reflect on the range of qualities of character and values the leaders and educators in this book found within themselves, consider which ones resonate for you. Which guide you in being authentically you as you face adversity? Think about ways in which you combine these values, or others, in ways that help you design learning and life.

adaptability: finding the ability to sit in the unknown and move forward anyway, embracing fresh perspectives from colleagues and people in different fields and investing in our own ability to adapt and grow

authenticity: being true to our own professional mission and to who we are, bringing our message to life through our actions

calm: intentionally creating an environment of peaceful calm, a haven of hope, not being reactive amid so many emotions

commitment: bouncing back when making mistakes and staying the course, striving to do right by students, teachers, and staff

compassion: being human with ourselves and one another, showing genuine concern and connecting with heart

courage: digging deep into a confidence that was not always there, breaking out of what was comfortable, taking risks, and finding possibilities we had not known existed

creativity: embracing fresh perspectives and finding new strategies in the face of both health and financial constraints

curiosity: looking at others without judgment or criticism but instead being curious and holding a sense of wonder about what is going on for others

empathy: listening and understanding the perspectives of others

equanimity: striving for evenness, awareness, trying not to be complacent and not to be reactive, holding strength alongside softness

flexibility: drawing upon practical problem-solving skills, rolling with the punches, understanding that everything is fluid, engaging in practical problem solving rather than responding from a place of fear

humility: remaining humble while still being self-confident, not letting our ego take over, especially as we achieve success

openness: sharing the truth of the challenges we face with staff and families, being clear and consistent with communication

passion: conveying our deep belief in our vision and approach, seeking to inspire and engage others in our belief in what is possible

patience: carefully taking one step at a time and having faith we will get through

perseverance: facing challenges, achieving successes, and also failing time and again, continuing to serve, not giving up, pushing on with the work even as it is emotionally, mentally, and physically exhausting

persistence: staying the course and being true to who we are and what we are doing

positivity: looking for the good, seeing the positive, and reframing situations to help people take on different perspectives

resilience: facing monumental adversity while bringing ourselves each and every day to serve, finding strength within ourselves and our communities so that we not only navigate through but find and further develop the best within ourselves and our communities

resourcefulness: thinking outside the box, using the resources we have inside of ourselves, being open to change, learning new things, welcoming challenges and problems because they will teach us

responsiveness: offering the programs and supports our communities need, being attuned and attentive to the specific needs of individuals

***sitzfleisch*:** a German term that literally means "sitting flesh"—sitting your bottom on the chair and getting things done

spirituality and mindfulness: feeling grounded in our sense of spirituality and in the present moment, practicing mindfulness meditation and gratitude

stubbornness: a determination to navigate through every challenge alongside an openness to advocate strongly for what could remain the same

vitality: bringing energy to our work, whether soft or enthusiastic, even when we are exhausted and overwhelmed

vulnerability: making mistakes publicly and apologizing, normalizing making mistakes without shame and the willingness to be vulnerable in a community

Being authentic during times of adversity as well as times of blessing, during major events and small, quiet moments, requires change. The gifts of growth arrive when we are open to getting to know ourselves better and are willing to surprise ourselves by what we find.

To be authentically ourselves is not a static process. It's a journey of change, of moving toward who we are capable of being. We can always choose to be attentive to our authentic selves and to the possibility of who we can become.

14

Budget and Busy-ness

A budget is a vision in numbers. A schedule is a vision in time.

Many times, in my leadership and in my life, the assertion that we spend our money and we spend our time on what we truly value has caused me to pause. It's revealed truths about myself that have made me proud and others that have made me cringe. Our budgets and our calendars are mirrors, revealing truths about ourselves that are aligned—or not—with who we aspire to be.

During the pandemic much was revealed in the way we managed money amid financial uncertainty and in the way we managed time amid overwhelming demands. Sadly, along with many other brick-and-mortar small businesses, many early childhood programs shut their doors forever during the challenging months of the pandemic. They were unable to survive the abrupt loss of income that came with governmental executive orders to shut down or go remote. K–12 schools for the most part fared better, keeping their students, albeit teaching them remotely. Yet there were numerous financial challenges for them as well. Those who came through stronger than before focused not only on learning and care but also on the business of running a school. Among the key factors in success were finding healthy ways to manage our budgets and healthy ways to manage our calendars.

Finance generally, and budgets specifically, emerged as a significant topic among those who not only navigated through the pandemic but got better. Key topics included navigating financial uncertainty; funding microschools, independent schools, and social impact programs; and providing equitable public education.

During the pandemic, time shifted. For some everything became far more intense. For others time slowed down. Time-related topics that emerged included being constantly on call, creating schedules that value leaders' time, and creating schedules that value kids' time.

Navigating Financial Uncertainty

In the frightening early days of the pandemic, I had what at the time felt like an ambitious goal for Discovery Village: I wanted to continue to exist as a business by New Year's Day, 2021. In many ways, the financial challenges we faced revealed vulnerabilities that have long existed for early childhood education. Child care is typically the second-highest expense for families, following only rent or mortgage. Teachers are notoriously, tragically poorly paid. And still, profit margins are razor thin. Creating budgets that reflect our values isn't easy.

When I closed my own center for just eight school days at the end of March 2020, budgeting was high on my list of priorities. I spent the week and a half we were closed consumed with two tasks. The first was drafting COVID health and safety protocols at a time when almost nobody had any guidance on doing so. The second was looking closely at finances, determining how long I could continue to operate with very minimal income coming in.

I watched with bated breath as Congress deliberated the first CARES Act. The legislation included the Paycheck Protection Program (PPP), which offered loans to small businesses. These loans could become fully forgiven grants if spent on approved expenses, primarily salaries but also rent or mortgage and utilities. When the legislation passed on Friday, March 27, 2020, I burst into tears of relief. I now had enough hope to reopen the following Monday. Until the PPP loan came through, I would cover payroll out of my savings.

Within hours of the PPP application becoming available through my bank, I applied. But funding ran out before my application could be processed. The day after learning I did not receive a loan was devastating for me. I let most of my staff know I had to furlough them, at least temporarily.

Still, I kept the center open. Two staff members and I taught in one room with six students. Soon Congress approved a second round of PPP loans. Seeking a lifeline, I learned all I could about both the PPP loan and the Economic Injury Disaster Loan (EIDL), both administered by the Small Business Administration. Seeing others struggle to access the help, I felt great sorrow. I went through a training program to assist others in applying for these loans. Additionally, I did my own research, beyond what the training offered, and created a list of lenders working with small businesses. I then reached out to local child care center owners and directors and ultimately assisted close to thirty local programs in obtaining loans. In addition to receiving the PPP and EIDL loans myself, I negotiated a rent relief plan with my landlord, postponing rent for June, July, and August 2020 until 2021. With those vital supports, I was able to keep our doors open.

Slowly, students returned. By June, thanks to a combination of the loans I received and the minimal amount of tuition still coming in, I could invite all furloughed staff members back. Some were frightened of contracting COVID-19 and opted not to return. Those who did come back took quantum leaps forward in improving the quality of our program. Many programs had similar experiences.

By spring 2021, after a dark winter of rising COVID-19 cases, the trickle of students returning transformed into a flood. Inquiries poured in and we were faced with a rapidly growing waiting list. Yet many of us, including my own center, could not hire sufficient staff. Within the next months we realized the problem would not be short-lived and that we were facing a very significant labor shortage. Classrooms had openings or even remained empty despite the many families who desperately wanted the spots for their children. Our attention turned to finding staff and increasing salaries while keeping child care affordable for families and remaining in business. Opening ourselves to new possibilities, we continued to look at income and spending, adjusting and readjusting continually.

Funding Microschools, Independent Schools, and Social Impact Programs

Funding microschools and independent schools is similar to funding early child care centers. In fact, early childhood programs frequently fit my definition of a microschool—a small school with a large vision for what learning can be. The highest expenses are for personnel and rent or mortgage, and these costs make affordability a significant challenge. Founders of these schools, and families considering them for their children, often talk about equity, longing to find ways to offer access to people who cannot afford hefty private school tuition.

Within pods, which formed quickly during the pandemic, educators and families intentionally kept overhead low. Many ran programs out of their home, without charging rent to the business. Some donated their time, leading their programs without taking any salary. While they gladly made the short-term investment, operating without paying salaries and rent or mortgage is not sustainable. Considering alternative sources of funding for microschools is a significant part of operating these innovative programs.

Randolph is categorized as an independent school and not a microschool per se. Nonetheless, it is a small school with a big vision. During the pandemic, Josh Kaplan, director of the Randolph School, designed a new tuition model in which families pay based on an algorithm determining what they can afford. The new model lessens distinctions between full-paying and scholarship students prevalent in many independent schools without reducing tuition revenue.

Other programs combined a range of approaches to maintain a healthy budget while serving their communities. This included offering sliding-scale tuition, fundraising, and grant writing.

Providing Equitable Public Education

As early childhood education programs, microschools, and social impact programs set out to serve as equitably as possible, public schools stood accountable for serving all children. It wasn't easy, and the many accomplishments of the public system deserve to be celebrated.

"There has been loss, but it hasn't been a lost year," Sara Lev of Larchmont Charter School in Los Angeles relayed. "Students showed resilience, flexibility, and real learning. I didn't know if kids could learn online. We did assessments, measured progress. They learned. We did some incredible things, and we are proud of that work. I will never forget these kids and families and the learning we did. It's strange to feel grateful."

Not only did public schools shift to remote learning, essentially overnight, but they also ensured that all children had internet access and a computer—requiring not an insignificant amount of money to be found and spent in short order. For children experiencing homelessness, the challenges were exacerbated. "COVID shed light on a lot of kids living at the poverty level," shared Bill Brennan, assistant superintendent for innovation and organizational development at the Farmingdale School District in New York. Public schools set out to do all they could, helping children access the technological tools necessary for remote learning. While grateful that his district entered the pandemic in a good financial situation, Bill focused on "how to make funding go a long way." He engaged teachers and administrators in gaining clarity on their goals.

Being Constantly on Call

As we looked closely at how we spent our money, we also needed to examine how we were spending our time. Navigating through the challenging months of the pandemic took its toll, with particular challenges for parents. "There was a serious blurring of lines between time on and time off," Sarah Damelin of Temple Beth Shalom said. "Saying you can do your work hours anytime sounds generous until looking at the hours and seeing how overwhelming it is to always be on call." She said she feels strongly there will need to be a pulling back from what she referred to as "on callness," being constantly on call both for work and as a mom.

Even before COVID, Joy Anderson struggled with the many demands of working full time, caring for her own children, and running her part-time passion project helping other moms start preschools. As the pandemic hit, Joy recognized how much her own children and her membership of preschool owners needed her. Wanting to be present for them, she realized she needed to quit her job and come home, giving her attention fully to her own family and to the owners of preschools she supports.

Coming out of those challenging days, many longed for a slower pace. "I am more careful with my time," shared Jess Durrett, whose son attends Muck and Wonder and who runs her own online tutoring business. "My days were packed with work and parenting in an unbalanced way. Having more time at home and focusing on establishing a safe space for my child really helped. The full days of work and school won't be part of us going forward. The hours in the day are too precious."

Creating Schedules That Value Leaders' Time

There was so much to do, for our work and for our families. And yes, some found in COVID the opportunity to slow down. Many, however, felt ourselves moving ever more quickly, finding the demands on us overwhelming.

Bill Brennan at the Farmingdale School District articulately put into words a question many of us were struggling with: How can we become masters of our own time? With that question front and center, Bill became very creative in blocking off times in his calendar for independent work, collaborative work during which people could schedule time with him, time to give back and contribute to the field, and time for his own learning. Bill found his calendar work so valuable, making it possible for him to be present for his community without being on call all the time, that he coached other leaders in his district to use a similar approach.

Many leaders learned to delegate more effectively, developing greater trust for each other and for their teams. "In the past I would want to do everything myself," Ashley Acers of Kaleidoscope said. But to navigate through the enormity of challenges her school faced, she had to let go of the need for control and trust her colleagues. Building Blocks Preschool owner Suzanne Gabli, relying on her team, explained how she pulled back from day-to-day operations of her school and focused on "the long-term, bigger picture, positioning her school for growth, preparing for growth."

Creating Schedules That Value Kids' Time

When Sara Lev's school went back to in-person learning, her administration divided Sara's transitional kindergarten class into two separate cohorts. One met in the morning and the other met in the afternoon. Students thus benefited from learning in a smaller group. From Sara's perspective, the experience was "amazing," she said. Children sustained greater stamina and energy for a half day than children in the past did in her full-day program. The positive results have led Sara to wonder whether this organization of schedules would be more effective for children in future years as well.

For years Mary Roux Train has observed the challenges working families face as their children move from full-time child care to the school hours of elementary school. "The school day doesn't fit the workday. It's antiquated," the school owner and teacher said. At Windsor Hill, she offers academics until 3:30 and then a wide range of enrichment programming until five o'clock. When families pick up their children at the end of the workday, they can just go home. There is no rushing to various after-school programs, and there is no homework.

Reclaiming family time was one of the significant rewards of Maria Ferrari's learning pod at Acton Academy Silicon Valley. When school ends at 3:30, "kids don't want to leave. They often stay till 4:30," Maria said. They can then go home, cook dinner with their families, or participate in sports or another activity if they choose to do so. There is no homework. "We've gotten time back as a family," she shared.

The Open School approach is grounded in self-directed learning, in which children have control over both their learning and their time. "There are few requirements for what they have to be doing," founder Cassandra Clausen explained. This includes some school meetings or meetings with their adviser. "The majority of the time they are doing what interests them."

In My Reflection Matters Village, "the schedule doesn't dominate learning. Kids decide if it is time to move on or dig deep," explained founder Chemay Morales-James. "It's a big weight off of parents' shoulders, as so many fights with kids are about schedules. There is flexibility around time."

Abilities and Possibilities

While others looked on or looked away as inequity gripped turn-of-the-twentieth-century Italy, Maria Montessori tackled the injustice she observed, confident in children's capacity to be independent thinkers and doers. Over the years, as the world faced two wars, Maria Montessori's vision expanded, and she emphasized peace.

As post–World War I Germany suffered, Rudolf Steiner laid a foundation for revitalization, championing a holistic approach to learning, life, and the task of rebuilding our nations and our world.

Amid the destruction and despair in Italy after World War II, Loris Malaguzzi built schools to prepare young children to fight against the oppression, injustice, and inequity of their future.

We are the future these visionary educators made possible.

These founders are all authentically and magnificently themselves. Their inspirational work crossed continents and generations. And, while powerfully distinct in many ways, the three share meaningful similarities. They were warriors, fighting against the injustice and brutality that marked so much of the experience of twentieth-century Europe. We stand on their shoulders.

Our world remains very much in turmoil yet simultaneously ripe with possibility. Like Montessori, Steiner, Malaguzzi, and so many other educators past and present, we can choose not to look away from the problems of our times. We can develop within ourselves the abilities needed to bring to life our visions of possibilities for our students and for ourselves, for our schools and for our world. The path forward is multifaceted. A variety of components are significant to our progress. These include prioritizing our own learning, including engaging in remote professional learning and receiving coaching and mentoring; reinventing our schools; creating new schools; and designing new models for learning.

Prioritizing Our Own Learning

"Professionally and personally, I'm putting in as much as my brain will take. I have enjoyed being a dry sponge soaking up information," Kaye Boehning, director of Tomorrow's Promise relayed with a sparkle in her eye. "I went from trying to save the business, from survival mode, to growing."

"Strength and a positive mindset" are invaluable assets Karina Wyllie of Koala Park Daycare said she relied on when the pandemic hit. Through personal development work over many years, Karina consistently has nurtured many abilities, including "determination, resilience, energy, vitality, positive outlook, open-mindedness, and adaptability," she said. She has attended training with well-known thought leaders Tony Robbins, Brendon Burchard, and numerous other mentors and participates in monthly life and business coaching. The learning has helped Karina embrace change and continuous improvement. "Every problem has a solution. Every problem is an opportunity to learn, an opportunity for change," Karina asserted. "Bad things will happen. You have to deal with things one day at a time, the best you can, with what you have. You have to know you tried, did your best. If you don't try, nothing will change or get better."

"Knowledge is a superpower," shared Karen Eilersen, founder and owner of Discovery Child Care Centre. "As a business owner it's important to position yourself with good people, other good leadership. You cannot do it alone. You need a team. You have to allow yourself the opportunity to be vulnerable, listen to others, and still be true to your vision."

"I am super excited to find opportunities to reach in new directions," said Mary Roux Train, cofounder of Windsor Hill. In recent years within her school district all of her professional development was connected to data and reporting. Launching out on her own, Mary has pursued many areas for growing her abilities, including a program at Harvard University for educators to design makerspaces and a collaboration with a new local children's museum.

Engaging in Remote Professional Learning

"Would I have been so comfortable with remote learning for adults had it not been for teaching children remotely?" asked transitional kindergarten teacher Sara Lev of Larchmont Charter School. While she couldn't say for sure, she did note that most of her learning and teaching adults has shifted online. For instance, Sara participated in a professional learning community focused on culturally responsive teaching with teacher educator and author Zaretta Hammond. Sara also facilitated at least two workshops a month for educators on early childhood project-based learning, noting that she had educators in her workshops from Pakistan, China, United Arab Emirates, and Taiwan.

"We gained a much deeper understanding and appreciation for online learning for adults," shared Alison Maher, executive director of Boulder Journey School. "We had been dreaming about an online master's for teachers but had many doubts." Bringing the master's program to fruition, as well as facilitating weekly virtual dialogues with hundreds of educators, showed Boulder Journey's staff how very powerful online learning, both formal and informal, can be.

Bill Brennan, an assistant superintendent at Farmingdale School District, shared that his district created a wide range of virtual professional development opportunities for staff. Cori Berg's staff at Hope Day School participated virtually in a national conference. She was able to bring in training programs from across the nation that would not have been accessible if not offered remotely.

Coaching and Mentoring

Joy Anderson, owner of Preschool System and Preschool All Stars Membership, knew she needed to find mentors to help her face the challenges ahead, as the floodgates of mothers interested in starting online preschools had been flung open. In addition to seeking training for herself, she realized she also needed a team. While it was "painful to let go of tasks and grow," Joy said she recognized she could not possibly do it all on her own, ultimately hiring ten new staff members.

A coach and a peer group helped Cassandra Clausen to see possibilities others couldn't. "I really learned the importance of a support network, especially of other leaders and founders who are action oriented," the Open School founder shared. She asked questions she wouldn't have otherwise considered and found solutions she wouldn't have even imagined. "I'm always curious, researching, and finding experts who can help," she said. "I'm always learning. I recommend everyone get a coach or mentor."

Reinventing Our Schools

When educators were required to shift to remote learning or operate with new health and safety protocols, change was not a choice. We could not continue operating our schools as though nothing had happened. We could not wait until we felt more prepared. Still, while change was required, many did far more than reluctantly acquiesce. Educators throughout the world embraced possibility in adversity, actively reinventing our programs.

From the earliest days of the pandemic, Boulder Journey School inspired others both by the example it set and by the connection and collaboration it nurtured. "Boulder Journey School has always been good at reinventing certain aspects of our work," relayed partner school program director Lauren Weatherly. "Thrust into this new reality, we see we can make changes so quickly, even when we don't have all the details worked out. COVID taught us to take action. Through virtual dialogues we found how to be more nimble but not perfectionist." Others at Boulder Journey School concurred. Community outreach specialist Alex Morgan shared, "There was a sense of freedom in not having to present as perfect." The results were inspirational. "We have increased quality and elevated the field, even without having all of the answers," Alison Maher said.

Creating New Schools

Some educators and parents found that the reinvention of the schools they had known was not enough. They needed new schools. Beginning very small, they used whatever resources they had. The visionary founders who began their own schools were not so unlike the villagers of Villa Cella in northern Italy, who built a preschool using land donated by a farmer and stones and bricks from bombed-out buildings. To build their schools, they donated their homes, their time, and their own money. Scrappy from the start, they found out that the essence of quality learning and care need not cost a lot.

It did not take long for these founders of today to think bigger, looking for spaces outside of their home and hiring more educators. Expenses grew and they designed funding models that would enable them to achieve their ambitious goals. How they would grow and how they might inspire others remained to be seen. As they stood at their own founding moments, they were joining a global conversation about what learning can be.

Mary Roux Train emotionally explained what many experienced: "You need to get to the core of your values and what you believe and follow your heart." Stepping out of what she had known was incredibly freeing for Mary. "I'm not an old teacher. I was just in an environment in which I was not able to be as creative and authentic to who I am as a teacher. This is the best way I feel I can make an impact," she said. Her experience resonated broadly as educators recognized that there are multiple pathways through which to make an impact. We can make choices for our learning, our careers, and our lives.

Designing New Models for Learning

Before COVID, My Reflection Matters Village didn't exist. Its precursor was, in the words of member Tamsyn Ambler, "basically a local homeschooling group," albeit designed specifically to serve BIPOC families. The village evolved into a space where modern-day civil rights can be pursued. "This is a space for our kids," she said. "It's not just anti-racist and antibias learning, inclusive of all, including gender-nonbinary children. It's not school. In the village, there is space to be constantly reflecting on when you are free, when you are controlled, and what's controlling you." There is also a substantial and continuously increasing amount of programming responsive to the interests of adults in the village. In many ways, the village has grown to be a place that serves the adults even more than it serves children. "I would say the village has been the best thing for my life. I'm grateful. I never imagined I would have this abundance," she said.

The Open School offers a model of what we can create when we open our minds to the possible. Its educators are designing a virtual international community of students, making their unique democratic approach accessible to learners throughout the world. In preparation, Cassandra Clausen and her team are thoughtful about nurturing relationships and facilitating robust engagement in the democratic learning model within a virtual environment. They are energized by the possibilities.

New models of learning are possible not only in small, agile programs but even in public education on a very large scale. Bill Brennan of the Farmingdale School District asserted, "Recognizing this as a transitional moment, people in my role, in any leadership role, need to do the inner work to maximize, optimize things so we can come out of transition with something a heck of a lot better. Normal may not have been that great. There is a big shift, and I don't know how public education will deal with it. There are now platforms in which anybody can teach. We need to find a way to harness those possibilities in order to maintain our relevance."

> Often you don't choose the challenge you face. The challenge chooses you.
>
> Frequently you don't choose the core value that can best guide you. The value chooses you.
>
> Still, you always have a choice.
>
> You can choose to embrace purpose and possibility.

Epilogue

The Journey Ahead

As the 2021–2022 school year began and I prepared to submit the final manuscript for this book, the highly contagious COVID-19 Delta variant was causing increasing levels of fear, uncertainty, and stress. There were so many stories of exhaustion, burnout, grief, and despair among educators. And yet, as in the spring of 2020 when the pandemic was new, educators, families, and kids were not only pulling through but finding ways to get better even amid the enormous challenge and adversity we were still facing. So many of us were persevering, committing to bringing forward powerful visions for learning, creating havens of hope in a world in need of so much healing, standing out by what we stand for.

There is so much in our world to stand for, and there is so much in our world to stand against. We have models from whom we can learn.

Maria Montessori stood for independence and peace.

Rudolf Steiner stood for holistic revitalization.

Loris Malaguzzi stood for justice and equity.

These educational visionaries, and so many others on whose shoulders we stand, were not primarily focused on college and career readiness. They would not accept standardization. They were fighting for a future in which independent thought, peace, revitalization, equity, and oppression would prevail over totalitarianism, war, devastation, despair, and injustice. They didn't act alone, nor did they act quickly. They were patient warriors, fighting battles that had not yet taken place, preparing the next generation for the challenge and adversity that might befall them.

We are that future for which they prepared, and we have a choice. We can revitalize our education system, design and build new schools, connect with aligned families and professionals, improve the quality of our programs, raise funds to make quality education accessible to all, create new approaches to learning, and so much more, all while designing lives of joy and purpose. Our next chapters are yet to be written.